# WELCOME!

**O**n behalf of Splash! Publications, we would like to welcome you to *The New England States*, one of several books in our U.S. Regions Series. Since this curriculum was designed by teachers, we are positive that you will find it to be the most useful program you have ever utilized to teach students about the New England states. We would like to take a few moments to familiarize you with the program.

## THE FORMAT

*The New England States* is a six lesson program covering each of the six New England states. Our goal is a curriculum that you can use the very first day you purchase our materials. No lessons to plan, comprehension questions to write, activities to create, or vocabulary words to define. Simply open the book and start teaching.

Each of the six lessons requires students to complete vocabulary cards, read about one of the six New England states, and complete a two-part Reading and Language comprehension activity that will expose them to various standardized test formats. In addition, each lesson includes a balanced mix of lower and higher level activities for students to complete. Vocabulary quizzes, cardinal and intermediate direction mapping, grid math, research projects and writing exercises utilizing graphic organizers like Venn Diagrams and Concept Webs, differentiating between primary and secondary sources, and cause and effect are the types of activities that will guide students through their journey of *The New England States*.

## THE LESSON PLANS

**O**n the next several pages, you will find the Lesson Plans for *The New England States*. The Lesson Plans clearly outline what students must do before, during, and after each lesson. Page numbers are listed so that you will immediately know what you need to photocopy before beginning each lesson. The answers to all activities, quizzes, and comprehension questions are located on pages 92-97.

**NOTE:** Students will complete a culminating activity at the end of the curriculum. We suggest that students keep the information from each lesson in a notebook or folder.

## THE VOCABULARY

Each lesson features words in bold type. We have included a Glossary on pages 86-91 to help students pronounce and define the words. Unlike a dictionary, the definitions in the Glossary are concise and written in context. Remember, we're teachers! Students will be exposed to these vocabulary words in the Reading and Language comprehension activities. They will also be tested on the vocabulary words five times throughout their study of *The New England States*.

Students will be responsible for filling out and studying the vocabulary cards. You may want to have students bring in a small box for storing their vocabulary cards. We don't have to tell you that incorporating these words into your Reading and Spelling programs will save time and make the words more meaningful for students.

## CORE STANDARDS: THE "BIG IDEAS"

Common Core Standards help teachers prioritize instruction and connect the "big ideas" students need to know in order to advance. Most states are already incorporating the Common Core Standards into their Learning Standards. As a reading-based program, *The New England States* fosters literacy in Social Studies.

At the same time that students are learning important factual content about the New England States, they are meeting the Common Core Standards for English Language Arts to make connections to the "big ideas" in American History. Common Core Standards found in *The New England States* have been noted in the Lesson Plans. Below is the legend used to abbreviate the Common Core Strands:

COMMON CORE STRAND CODE:
CC = COMMON CORE
RL = READING-LITERATURE
RI = READING INFORMATIONAL TEXT
RF = READING FOUNDATIONS SKILLS
W = WRITING
SL = SPEAKING LISTENING
L = LANGUAGE

## THE AUDIO CDs

*The New England States* includes two Audio CDs. They can be found in the CD sleeves in the back of this book. Each of the six lessons has been professionally recorded word-for-word. Learning about history involves a tremendous amount of reading and we hope that having the curriculum in audio format will help facilitate this process.

## THE COPYRIGHT

# OUR OTHER TITLES

### COMPLETE STATE HISTORY PROGRAMS
*Do American History!*
*Do Arizona!*
*Do California!*
*Do Colorado!*
*Do Florida!*
*Do Nevada!*
*Do New Mexico!*
*Do Texas!*
*Do Washington!*

### LITERATURE STUDY GUIDES
*Charlotte's Web*
*Cricket in Times Square*
*Enormous Egg*
*Sarah, Plain and Tall*

### PRIMARY SERIES
*Leveled Math: Addition*
*Leveled Math: Subtraction*
*National Holidays*
*National Symbols*
*Poems for Every Holiday*
*Poems for Every Season*

### AMERICAN HISTORY SERIES
*New World Explorers*
*Spanish Explorers & Conquistadors*
*The Thirteen Original Colonies*
*Early American Government*
*The American Revolution*
*Slavery in America*
*The Civil War*
*Westward Expansion*

### U.S. REGION SERIES
*The Middle Atlantic States*
*The Great Lakes States*
*The Great Plains States*
*The Southeast States*
*The Southwest States*
*The Mountain States*
*The Pacific States*

### STATE HISTORY SERIES
*Arizona Geography*
*Arizona Animals*
*Arizona History*
*Arizona Government & Economy*
*California Geography*
*California Animals*
*California History*
*California Government & Economy*
*Florida Geography*
*Florida Animals*
*Florida History*
*Florida Government & Economy*
*Illinois History*
*Indiana History*
*Michigan History*
*Ohio History*
*Texas Geography*
*Texas Animals*
*Texas History*
*Texas Government & Economy*

# TABLE OF CONTENTS

## THE NEW ENGLAND STATES

# TABLE OF CONTENTS

## THE NEW ENGLAND STATES (CONTINUED)

# ★ LESSONS at a GLANCE ★

**1.** Before reading Connecticut, students will:
- complete Vocabulary Cards for *abolished, accused, adopted, agriculture, allies, American Revolution, ammunition, antislavery, appointed, Bermuda, borders, capital, charter, citizens, colonies, colonists, Confederate States of America, conflict, constitution, Continental Army, contrast, debt, dominion, economy, elections, England, Europeans, exotic, governor, Great Britain, Great Lakes, historians, imported, independent, industries, inhabited, island, loyal, mammals, mansion, manufacturing, mother country, motto, Netherlands, New England, New World, North America, overthrown, plantations, profitable, Puritan, seceded, surrendered, sustains, territories, textile, transplanted, treaty, trolley, Union, united, vowed, wampum.* (pg. 1)

After reading Connecticut (*pps. 2-11*), students will:
- answer Connecticut Reading Comprehension Questions. (pg. 12)
- complete Connecticut Language Skills Exercise. (pg. 13)
- fill in Connecticut and its state capital on the New England Study Guide. (pg. 14)
- create a Venn Diagram comparing the Civil War and Revolutionary War. (pps. 15-16)
- use Venn Diagram to write a Compare and Contrast paragraph. (pg. 17)
- take a Vocabulary Quiz for New England States Part I. (pps. 18-19)

THE CONNECTICUT LESSON COVERS THESE 5TH GRADE CORE STANDARDS:
CC.5.RI.4, CC.5.RI.7, CC.5.RI.10, CC.5.RF.3A, CC.5.RF.4A, CC.5.RF.4C, CC.5.L.4A, CC.5.L.4C, CC.5.L.6

# Lessons at a Glance

**2.** Before reading Maine, students will:
- complete Vocabulary Cards for *autobiography, biographies, coast, compromise, confederacy, conquered, debate, defeated, explorations, fertilized, harsh, maize, merchants, muskets, New France, Parliament, populated, raided, species, timber, victorious, voyages, West Indies.* *(pg. 1)*

After reading Maine *(pps. 20-24)*, students will:
- answer Maine Reading Comprehension Questions. *(pg. 25)*
- complete Maine Language Skills Exercise. *(pg. 26)*
- fill in Maine and its state capital on the New England Study Guide. *(pg. 14)*
- differentiate between primary and secondary sources. *(pg. 27)*
- take a Vocabulary Quiz for New England States Part II. *(pps. 28-29)*

THE MAINE LESSON COVERS THESE 5TH GRADE CORE STANDARDS:
CC.5.RI.4, CC.5.RI.7, CC.5.RI.10, CC.5.RF.3A, CC.5.RF.4A, CC.5.RF.4C, CC.5.L.4A, CC.5.L.4C, CC.5.L.6

# ★ LESSONS *at a* GLANCE ★

**3.** Before reading Massachusetts, students will:
- complete Vocabulary Cards for *boycotting, branded, canal, Continental Congress, delegates, devoted, disguised, evacuated, flee, geography, harbor, hostility, intolerable, liberty, massacre, militia, minutemen, monuments, peninsula, Pilgrims, preserved, protest, reenactment, repealed, representatives, resort, seaport, survival, venison. (pg. 1)*

After reading Massachusetts *(pps. 30-36)*, students will:
- answer Massachusetts Reading Comprehension Questions. *(pg. 37)*
- complete Massachusetts Language Skills Exercise. *(pg. 38)*
- fill in Massachusetts and its state capital on the New England Study Guide. *(pg. 14)*
- use number pairs to complete Massachusetts Grid Math. *(pps. 39-41)*
- take a Vocabulary Quiz for New England States Part III. *(pps. 42-43)*

THE MASSACHUSETTS LESSON COVERS THESE 5TH GRADE CORE STANDARDS:
**CC.5.RI.4, CC.5.RI.7, CC.5.RI.10, CC.5.RF.3A, CC.5.RF.4A, CC.5.RF.4C, CC.5.L.4A, CC.5.L.4C, CC.5.L.6**

# LESSONS *at a* GLANCE

**4.** Before reading New Hampshire, students will:
  • complete Vocabulary Cards for ***boundaries, captive, commerce, Confederacy, council, destructive, expanding, expedition, formations, founded, glacial, granite, illegal, interior, livestock, privateers, production, prospering, province, recovered, scalps.*** *(pg. 1)*

After reading New Hampshire *(pps. 44-51)*, students will:
  • answer New Hampshire Reading Comprehension Questions. *(pg. 52)*
  • complete New Hampshire Language Skills Exercise. *(pg. 53)*
  • fill in New Hampshire and its state capital on the New England Study Guide. *(pg. 14)*
  • create a New Hampshire Concept Web and write an expository paragraph. *(pg. 54)*
  • take a Vocabulary Quiz for New England States Part IV. *(pps. 55-56)*

THE NEW HAMPSHIRE LESSON COVERS THESE 5TH GRADE CORE STANDARDS:
CC.5.RI.4, CC.5.RI.7, CC.5.RI.10, CC.5.RF.3A, CC.5.RF.4A, CC.5.RF.4C, CC.5.L.4A, CC.5.L.4C, CC.5.L.6

# LESSONS *at a* GLANCE

**5.**  Before reading Rhode Island, students will:
- complete Vocabulary Cards for *abolitionist, annual, artifacts, donations, exhibits, federal, gorge, habitats, kayaking, mansions, nationalities, official, planetarium, Quaker, ratify, refuge, revolt, solo, synagogue, varieties, wilderness, yacht.* *(pg. 1)*

After reading Rhode Island *(pps. 57-61),* students will:
- answer Rhode Island Reading Comprehension Questions. *(pg. 62)*
- complete Rhode Island Language Skills Exercise. *(pg. 63)*
- fill in Rhode Island and its state capital on the New England Study Guide. *(pg. 14)*
- use cardinal and intermediate directions to plot points of interest on a New England Map. *(pps. 64-69)*

THE RHODE ISLAND LESSON COVERS THESE 5TH GRADE CORE STANDARDS:
CC.5.RI.4, CC.5.RI.7, CC.5.RI.10, CC.5.RF.3A, CC.5.RF.4A, CC.5.RF.4C, CC.5.W.7, CC.5.W.10, CC.5.L.4A, CC.5.L.4C, CC.5.L.6

# LESSONS at a GLANCE

**6.** Before reading Vermont, students will:
- complete Vocabulary Cards for *artillery, climate, convinced, disputes, forbid, innocent, Mormon, outlaws, potash, tavern, tourism, vicious.* *(pg. 1)*

After reading Vermont *(pps. 70-74)*, students will:
- answer Vermont Reading Comprehension Questions. *(pg. 75)*
- complete Vermont Language Skills Exercise. *(pg. 76)*
- fill in Vermont and its state capital on the New England Study Guide. *(pg. 14)*
- read about the Revolutionary War and answer cause and effect questions. *(pps. 77-79)*
- solve riddles about the six New England States. *(pps. 80-82)*
- take a Vocabulary Quiz for New England States Part V. *(pps. 83-84)*
- take the New England States and Capitals Quiz. *(pg. 85)*

THE VERMONT LESSON COVERS THESE 5TH GRADE CORE STANDARDS:
CC.5.RI.4, CC.5.RI.7, CC.5.RI.10, CC.5.RF.3A, CC.5.RF.4A, CC.5.RF.4C, CC.5.W.1B, CC.5.SL.1A, CC.5.SL.1C, CC.5.L.4A, CC.5.L.4C, CC.5.L.6

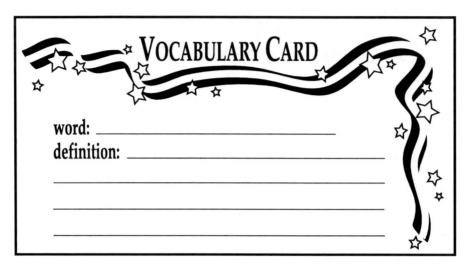

## VOCABULARY CARD

word: _____

definition: _____

_____

_____

_____


## VOCABULARY CARD

word: _____

definition: _____

_____

_____

_____


## VOCABULARY CARD

word: _____

definition: _____

_____

_____

_____

# CONNECTICUT

Connecticut, the Constitution State, was one of the original 13 **colonies** in America. It is the southernmost of the **New England** states in the Northeast region of the United States.

In 1639, **colonists** in Connecticut **adopted** the nation's first written **constitution**. This is why Connecticut is nicknamed the Constitution State.

The name Connecticut comes from a group of Native Americans who spoke the Algonquian (al•GONG•kee•in) language. The name means "up the long river." The river is the Connecticut River. The Connecticut River runs through the middle of Connecticut, dividing the state in half.

The **capital** and second largest city in Connecticut is Hartford. Hartford is located on the west bank of the Connecticut River. It is a major **manufacturing** city in Connecticut.

The state bird of Connecticut is the American Robin. The state flower is the Mountain Laurel, and the state tree is the White Oak. Connecticut's **motto** is "He Who **Transplanted** Still **Sustains**."

## CONNECTICUT'S POINTS OF INTEREST

There are more than 100 state parks and forests in Connecticut. Hikers enjoy the Appalachian (ap•uh•LAY•shun) Trail, which crosses through western Connecticut. The Beardsley Zoological Gardens in Bridgeport are home to **mammals** and **exotic** rain forest animals of **North America**. The Connecticut River invites visitors who enjoy fishing, boating, and swimming.

There are also many public beaches on Long **Island** Sound. Long Island Sound is an enclosed area of the Atlantic Ocean that **borders** Connecticut on the south. This area of water separates Long Island, New York from the Connecticut shore.

Like the other New England states, Connecticut is also rich in history. There are hundreds of historic homes and battle sites throughout the state. Mystic Seaport Museum is a world famous museum that shows visitors what life was like in a whaling village during the 1800s. There is a working steam-powered railroad in the town of Essex and **trolley** museums in East Windsor and Branford.

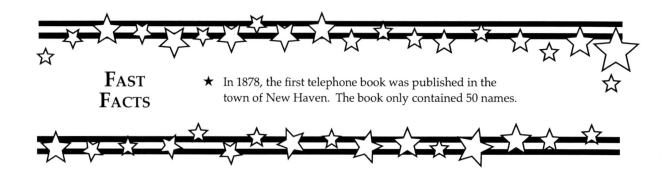

**FAST FACTS**

★ In 1878, the first telephone book was published in the town of New Haven. The book only contained 50 names.

## CONNECTICUT'S FIRST PEOPLE

Native Americans **inhabited** Connecticut long before any other people visited the area. They spoke the Algonquian language and included the Pequot (PEE•kwat), the Mohegan (mo•HEE•gun), the Niantic (nye•AN•tick), and the Siwanog (SEE•wah•nog).

The Pequot was the most powerful and feared Algonquian tribe. In the early 1600s, there were about 20,000 Native Americans living in Connecticut. They survived by hunting deer, fishing, and farming corn, beans, and tobacco. Native Americans in Connecticut lived in wigwams. These were dome-shaped houses made of poles, tree bark, and grass.

During the 1600s, **Europeans** arrived in Connecticut. **Historians** believe that the first white explorer in Connecticut was Adriaen Block. He was a Dutchman from the **Netherlands**. The Dutch were not really interested in establishing permanent settlements in Connecticut. They were interested in trading with the Native Americans.

The Dutch gave the Native Americans European tools and metal weapons. In return, the Native Americans gave the Dutch beaver furs. The furs were taken back to Europe where they were sold for a very high price. Hats and other pieces of clothing were made out of the beaver furs. To protect their **profitable** fur trade from other European groups, the Dutch built a fort in the present-day city of Hartford.

## THOMAS HOOKER

Thomas Hooker was a **Puritan** preacher. He was born in **England**. In 1633, Hooker traveled to America in search of religious freedom. In America, Thomas Hooker settled in Massachusetts, but he did not always agree with the colony's leaders.

Hooker believed that each church should be **independent**. He also felt that the people of each church had the right to choose the colony's leaders and decide what powers those leaders should have.

The leaders in Massachusetts disagreed with Hooker. They felt that only the leaders of the Puritan church should choose leaders for the colony.

In 1636, Thomas Hooker and a group of 100 colonists left Massachusetts. They moved to Connecticut and started a new colony. Hooker made positive changes in his colony. All church members, not just church leaders, chose the colony's leaders.

**THOMAS HOOKER**

Together with other English colonists who moved from Massachusetts, Hooker's group built the towns of Hartford, Wethersfield, and Windsor. These towns were called the "Three River Towns" because they were built along the Connecticut River.

Most of the Native Americans were friendly to the English colonists living in Connecticut. Instead of just taking the land from the Native Americans, Hooker and his followers purchased the land in Connecticut.

## THE PEQUOT WAR

During the 1630s, two things happened that destroyed the peace between Connecticut's Native Americans and the colonists. Control of the fur trade was the first struggle. The Pequot controlled the fur trade throughout New England. They decided which tribes could trade with the white settlers and the price that would be paid for the furs. The Pequot refused to allow the colonists to control the **wampum** and fur trade in New England. This made the colonists very angry.

In 1634 and 1636, colonists killed two members of the Pequot tribe. The Pequot captured the murderers and refused to let them go. Fighting broke out after a colonist **accused** a Pequot of murder. The colonists declared war on the Pequot. The Pequot War was the first major **conflict** between the colonists in the **New World** and the Native Americans.

With the help of the Narragansett (nar•ra•GAN•set) and Mohegan tribes, the colonists attacked the main Pequot village. They burned the Pequot village and killed Native American men, women, and children as they tried to escape. The Pequot who survived were captured and taken to **Bermuda** where they were sold into slavery.

## THE FIRST CONSTITUTION

In 1639, the people of the Three River Towns **united** as one colony. They formed their own set of laws called the Fundamental Orders of Connecticut. This was the first written constitution in the New World. The Fundamental Orders established an independent government that made laws for **elections**, courts, powers of officials, and taxes. It gave all men who owned land the right to vote.

## CONTROL OF CONNECTICUT

In 1662, Charles II was the king of England. King Charles II established Connecticut as an independent colony. He also gave the Connecticut Colony a **charter**. The charter allowed the colonists more control over their government. King Charles II allowed the Connecticut Colony to have control of all land in present-day Connecticut.

In 1685, King Charles II died. His brother, James II, became the king of England. King James II wanted more control over the colonies in America. He took away Connecticut's power to rule itself. In 1686, King James II united Connecticut with other nearby colonies. The new colony was called the **Dominion** of New England.

King James II **appointed** a royal **governor** for the Dominion of New England. His name was Sir Edmund Andros. In 1687, Andros demanded that Connecticut give up its charter. The leaders of Connecticut refused. They hid Connecticut's charter in a hollow oak tree. This tree became known as the Charter Oak. It stood for Connecticut's love of freedom.

By 1689, King James II had been **overthrown** and the colonists sent Sir Edmund Andros back to England. Connecticut once again became a separate colony.

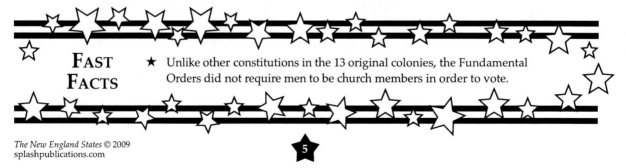

**FAST FACTS**  ★ Unlike other constitutions in the 13 original colonies, the Fundamental Orders did not require men to be church members in order to vote.

# THE FUR TRADE

The colonists from England were not the only settlers in the New World. While the English colonists established permanent settlements along the Atlantic Ocean, the French colonists settled in the **Great Lakes** area.
Both groups were interested in gaining more land for their countries and taking control of the beaver hunting and trading **territories**.

Beaver furs were worth a lot of money to the colonists. The furs were shipped back to France and England where they were sold for a very high profit. Everyone in these countries wanted a beautiful hat made of beaver fur. The French and English would do anything to protect this business.

Native Americans in the Great Lakes area trapped beaver and traded with the French colonists. Native Americans in the Northeast region trapped and traded with the English colonists.

The beaver trade was just as important to the Native Americans. Through trade with the French and English colonists, the Native Americans received weapons and metal tools they had never seen before. The Native Americans were also willing to do anything to protect the beaver business.

# THE FRENCH AND INDIAN WAR

**B**attles over beaver hunting territories were common. As all of the beaver in one area was captured, the Native Americans moved to another territory. Many times this hunting territory already belonged to another group of Native Americans. Fighting broke out and the strongest group usually won.

The French and Indian War was the biggest battle fought to protect land and beaver hunting territories. Beginning in 1754, the French colonists and their Native American **allies** battled the English colonists and their Native American allies. The fighting lasted for nine long years. No battles took place on Connecticut's soil, but more than 5,000 men from Connecticut fought against the French.

In 1763, the French and Indian War ended. France and their Native American allies lost. France signed a **treaty** with **Great Britain**. The treaty required France to give up all of its land in America east of the Mississippi River.

## GREAT BRITAIN'S TAXES

Fighting the French and Indian War was very expensive for Great Britain. Sending soldiers and weapons from Great Britain to America was costly. Protecting the colonists from Native American attacks after the war was also expensive.

Great Britain felt that the colonists should pay for these things. After all, they were living in America. The people of Great Britain certainly couldn't be expected to pay for battles and protection that didn't affect them.

Great Britain chose to tax the English colonists living in America to pay for these things. The Sugar Act placed a tax on **imported** items like sugar, molasses, and wine. The Stamp Act raised money by taxing all kinds of documents printed in the colonies. This included newspapers, calendars, and legal papers.

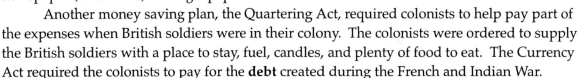

Another money saving plan, the Quartering Act, required colonists to help pay part of the expenses when British soldiers were in their colony. The colonists were ordered to supply the British soldiers with a place to stay, fuel, candles, and plenty of food to eat. The Currency Act required the colonists to pay for the **debt** created during the French and Indian War.

## THE AMERICAN REVOLUTION

The colonists refused to buy the taxed items or give the British soldiers food and shelter. To punish the colonists, Great Britain passed laws that took away the colonists' freedom to make their own laws.

The colonists grew tired of Great Britain's demands. They had always been **loyal** to their **mother country**, but now they wanted to be independent and make their own rules and laws. Great Britain refused to give the colonists their freedom. In 1775, the English colonists in America declared war. The first shots of the **American Revolution** were fired in the New England town of Lexington, Massachusetts.

## NATHAN HALE

Nathan Hale was born in Connecticut on June 6, 1755. At the beginning of the Revolutionary War, young Nathan Hale was only 20 years old. Although Hale was a successful teacher, he quickly volunteered to fight for American independence.

Hale's leadership in several early battles gained him rank as a captain in the **Continental Army**. Within a short time, he earned himself a place in the Rangers. The Rangers were known for their daring leadership and fighting qualities in dangerous missions.

General George Washington, commander of the Continental Army, asked the Rangers' commander to select a man to spy on the British soldiers. The mission required someone very brave who would risk his life to bring back information. Nathan Hale volunteered for the dangerous mission.

Dressed as a Dutch school teacher, Hale easily crossed the British lines. He spied on the British and got the information that General Washington needed. He was captured by British soldiers as he returned to the American lines.

General William Howe, commander of the British Army, sentenced Nathan Hale to death. Just before he was hanged, it was reported that 21 year old Nathan Hale said, "I only regret that I have but one life to lose for my country."

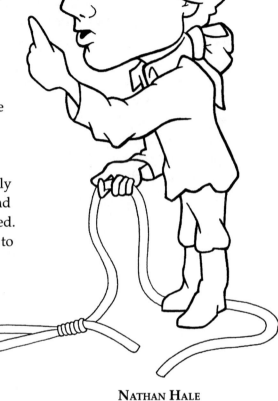

NATHAN HALE

## INDEPENDENCE FROM GREAT BRITAIN

Nathan Hale and the thousands of other men from Connecticut who fought for freedom did not die needlessly. In 1776, the colonies declared their independence from Great Britain. The 13 original colonies formed a new nation that they named the United States of America. In 1781, Great Britain **surrendered** the war to the United States. In 1783, the United States and Great Britain signed a peace treaty. Five years later, on January 9, 1788, Connecticut became the fifth state to join the new **Union**.

## CONNECTICUT'S ECONOMY

During Connecticut's colonial days, its **economy** was based on **agriculture**. After Connecticut became a state, it began manufacturing brass products, clocks, and rubber products. In the 1800s, **textile** mills and shipbuilding were also important **industries** in Connecticut.

Connecticut's economy was very different from the economy in the Southern colonies and states. Southerners were farmers who built huge cotton and tobacco **plantations**. The Southern farmers purchased black slaves from Africa to plant and pick their crops.

## SLAVERY IN THE UNITED STATES

The black slaves became the property of the Southern farmers. The slaves did not have any of the freedoms enjoyed by white people in the United States. Slaves were not paid for their work. They were not allowed to leave the plantations, purchase property of their own, or make any of their own decisions. Slave owners, or "masters,"

**TOBACCO PLANT**

were completely in control of them until the slaves died. Even a slave's children belonged to the master of the plantation. Children of black slaves were not allowed to go to school or learn to read and write like white children.

In the Northern states, like Connecticut, there were very few large farms. Some Northerners did own slaves, but most of the nation's slaves were in the South. Most people in the Northern states believed that owning slaves was cruel. The Northerners wanted to end slavery in the United States. The people in the South disagreed. Southern farmers argued that they needed slaves to work for them on their huge plantations. If slavery was **abolished**, the Southern states planned to separate from the Union.

# HARRIET BEECHER STOWE

In 1811, Harriet Beecher was born in Connecticut. Her father, Lyman Beecher, was a preacher and a leader in the **antislavery** movement. Through her father's teachings in church and at home, Harriet learned to hate slavery.

In 1836, Harriet married Calvin Stowe. He was a professor who was also against slavery. They often gave shelter to runaway slaves who escaped North to freedom.

Though Calvin and Harriet were white, they knew the pain that a black woman felt when her child was sold at a slave auction. Four of their own seven children died of illness or disease.

Harriet began writing at the age of 13. At the age of 41, she wrote her most famous book, *Uncle Tom's Cabin*. This book followed the lives of slaves as they were sold into slavery, beaten to death, or separated from their families at slave auctions.

*Uncle Tom's Cabin* was the most powerful attack on slavery written in the 1850s. It sold 3,000 copies on the first day it was published. More copies of *Uncle Tom's Cabin* were sold than any other book except the Bible.

*Uncle Tom's Cabin* was read by so many people that it scared slave owners. They feared that people would feel sorry for the slaves and refuse to return runaway slaves to their masters. That is exactly what happened.

**HARRIET BEECHER STOWE**

After Harriet Beecher Stowe's book was published, more people helped slaves escape to freedom. When President Abraham Lincoln met Harriet Beecher Stowe he said, "So you're the little lady who started the Civil War!"

# THE CIVIL WAR

In 1860, Abraham Lincoln was elected president of the United States. President Lincoln **vowed** to end slavery. The Southern states kept their promise and separated from the Union. In 1861, eleven Southern states in the Union **seceded** and formed a new nation. They called their nation the **Confederate States of America**. They formed the Confederate Army and prepared to fight the 23 states in the North who were still part of the Union. On April 12, 1861, the first shots of the Civil War were fired in South Carolina.

During the Civil War, 55,000 men from Connecticut fought for the Union Army to end slavery and bring the United States back together. Connecticut's industries helped the war effort by providing blankets, firearms, **ammunition**, and ships for the Civil War.

In 1865, the Civil War ended. Slavery was abolished in the United States. All states were required to free their slaves. The Southern states were not permitted to rejoin the Union until they wrote new constitutions that gave black **citizens** the same rights and freedoms as white citizens. It took five long years after the end of the Civil War for all 11 Southern states to be readmitted to the Union.

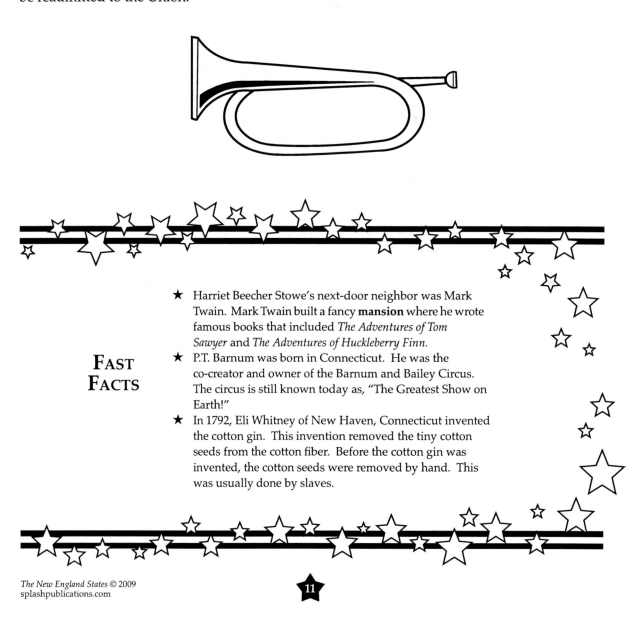

## FAST FACTS

★ Harriet Beecher Stowe's next-door neighbor was Mark Twain. Mark Twain built a fancy **mansion** where he wrote famous books that included *The Adventures of Tom Sawyer* and *The Adventures of Huckleberry Finn*.

★ P.T. Barnum was born in Connecticut. He was the co-creator and owner of the Barnum and Bailey Circus. The circus is still known today as, "The Greatest Show on Earth!"

★ In 1792, Eli Whitney of New Haven, Connecticut invented the cotton gin. This invention removed the tiny cotton seeds from the cotton fiber. Before the cotton gin was invented, the cotton seeds were removed by hand. This was usually done by slaves.

# CONNECTICUT

**Directions:** Read each question. Darken the circle for the correct answer.

**Directions:** Darken the circle for the word that has the same or almost the same meaning as the underlined word.

1   The name Connecticut means "up the long river." The river is –

   A   the Mississippi River
   B   the Missouri River
   C   the Connecticut River
   D   the Snake River

2   According to the information about Connecticut, why did Thomas Hooker travel to America?

   F   He was paid by Great Britain.
   G   He was searching for religious freedom.
   H   He needed a job.
   J   He wanted to be the first European to travel across the Atlantic Ocean.

3   The boxes below show events from Connecticut's history.

| In 1639, the Three Rivers Towns formed the Fundamental Orders of Connecticut. | | In 1763, the French and Indian War ended. |
|---|---|---|
| 1 | 2 | 3 |

Which event belongs in the second box?

   A   Nathan Hale fought in the Revolutionary War.
   B   Connecticut became the fifth state to join the Union.
   C   The Connecticut colony became part of the Dominion of England.
   D   The Pequot War was fought.

4   <u>Accused</u> means –

   F   blamed
   G   honored
   H   forgiven
   J   questioned

5   <u>Conflict</u> means –

   A   agreement
   B   struggle
   C   happiness
   D   trust

6   <u>United</u> means –

   F   separated
   G   angered
   H   closed
   J   joined

7   <u>Debt</u> means –

   A   money earned
   B   money paid
   C   money stolen
   D   money owed

8   <u>Surrendered</u> means –

   F   gave up
   G   joined
   H   forgave
   J   punished

**READING**

**Answers**

1  Ⓐ Ⓑ Ⓒ Ⓓ     5  Ⓐ Ⓑ Ⓒ Ⓓ
2  Ⓕ Ⓖ Ⓗ Ⓙ     6  Ⓕ Ⓖ Ⓗ Ⓙ
3  Ⓐ Ⓑ Ⓒ Ⓓ     7  Ⓐ Ⓑ Ⓒ Ⓓ
4  Ⓕ Ⓖ Ⓗ Ⓙ     8  Ⓕ Ⓖ Ⓗ Ⓙ

Directions: Read each sentence carefully. Darken the circle for the correct answer to each question.

After reading about Connecticut, you decide to write a report about Nathan Hale.

**1** Which of these topics should <u>not</u> be included in your report?

   **A** Nathan Hale's childhood.

   **B** The causes of the French and Indian War.

   **C** Nathan Hale's leadership in the Continental Army.

   **D** Nathan Hale's bravery.

You need to use a dictionary to look up some words to use in your report. Use these entries to answer questions 2 and 3.

---

A•mer•i•can Rev•o•lu•tion *n.* Conflict between 13 English colonies in North America and their mother country, Great Britain. Also known as the Revolutionary War.

Con•ti•nen•tal Ar•my *n.* American troops that fought against Great Britain during the Revolutionary War.

moth•er coun•try *n.* Original homeland of the English colonists.

loy•al *n.* Faithful.

---

**2** How can the entries be changed so that they are in alphabetical order?

   **F** Put <u>mother country</u> after <u>American Revolution.</u>

   **G** Put <u>loyal</u> after <u>American Revolution.</u>

   **H** Put <u>Continental Army</u> first.

   **J** Put <u>loyal</u> before <u>mother country.</u>

**3** Which guide words might mark the page on which you would find the word <u>loyal</u>?

   **A** laugh-lawyer

   **B** lost-lumpy

   **C** live-lovely

   **D** look-loser

Study this Table of Contents from a book about Nathan Hale. Then answer questions 4-6.

---

### Table of Contents

---

**4** Which chapter should you read to learn about Nathan Hale's Death?

   **F** Chapter 1

   **G** Chapter 2

   **H** Chapter 3

   **J** Chapter 4

**5** On which page does Chapter 3 end?

   **A** 7

   **B** 8

   **C** 14

   **D** 19

**6** Chapter 1 might contain information about all of these things <u>except</u> –

   **F** the moments before Nathan Hale was hanged

   **G** Nathan's childhood friends

   **H** the date of Nathan's birth

   **J** the name of Nathan Hale's fifth grade teacher

---

LANGUAGE

**Answers**

1 Ⓐ Ⓑ Ⓒ Ⓓ     4 Ⓕ Ⓖ Ⓗ Ⓙ

2 Ⓕ Ⓖ Ⓗ Ⓙ     5 Ⓐ Ⓑ Ⓒ Ⓓ

3 Ⓐ Ⓑ Ⓒ Ⓓ     6 Ⓕ Ⓖ Ⓗ Ⓙ

# NEW ENGLAND
## STATES AND CAPITALS STUDY GUIDE

During this unit, you will be studying about each of the six New England states. In this activity, you will create a study guide to help you take a quiz about the New England states and their capitals.

**Directions:** Use the blank map of the New England states to make a study guide. As you learn about each state, find the state on the map. Label each state with its correct name. On the lines provided, fill in each state's capital city. Spelling Counts!

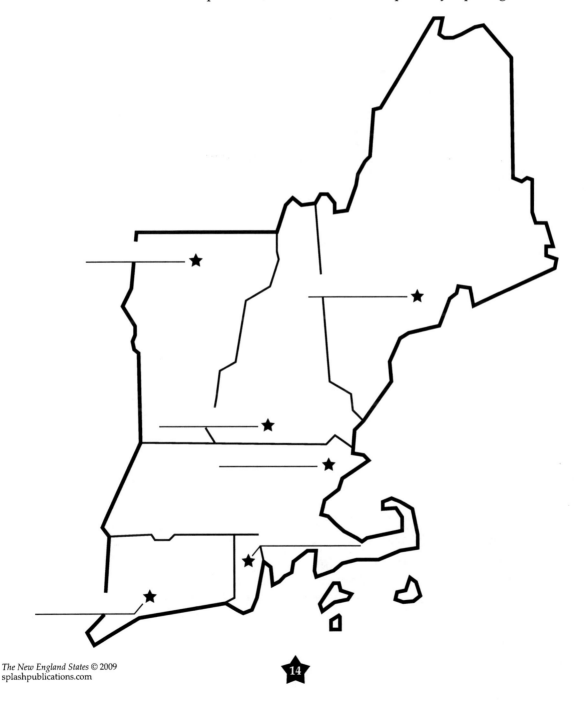

# MAKING A VENN DIAGRAM

**A** Venn Diagram is a great tool to use when you want to create a graphic that shows how topics are different, yet alike at the same time. In a Venn Diagram, two or more large circles overlap in the middle. The differences between the chosen topics are written in the large outer areas of the circles. Things that the topics have in common are written where the circles overlap.

Look at the Venn Diagram below. There are two large circles that overlap to show how Nathan Hale and Harriet Beecher Stowe were both different and alike. In the large areas of the circles, the differences between Nathan Hale and Harriet Beecher Stowe have been listed. The overlapping sections of the circles list the ways that Nathan Hale and Harriet Beecher Stowe were alike.

TOPIC: _____Nathan Hale_____    TOPIC: _____Harriet Beecher Stowe_____

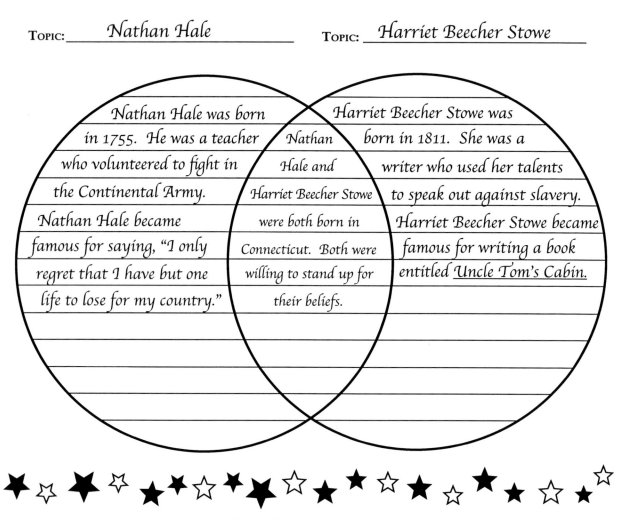

Nathan Hale was born in 1755. He was a teacher who volunteered to fight in the Continental Army. Nathan Hale became famous for saying, "I only regret that I have but one life to lose for my country."

Nathan Hale and Harriet Beecher Stowe were both born in Connecticut. Both were willing to stand up for their beliefs.

Harriet Beecher Stowe was born in 1811. She was a writer who used her talents to speak out against slavery. Harriet Beecher Stowe became famous for writing a book entitled Uncle Tom's Cabin.

**Directions:** In this activity, you will use the Venn Diagram on the next page to compare and **contrast** the Civil War and the American Revolution. Use the information from Connecticut as well as other books, encyclopedias, and the Internet to find the information for your Venn Diagram. Follow the example by listing the differences between the two wars in the large areas of the circles. Use the overlapping areas of the circles to list ways that the Civil War and the American Revolution were alike.

TOPIC: _____ The American Revolution

TOPIC: _____ The Civil War

The first shots of the American Revolution were fired in Massachusetts.

The first shots of the Civil War were fired in South Carolina.

Both wars were fought in the present-day United States.

# ═☆═☆═ Compare & Contrast Paragraph ═☆═☆═

**Directions:** Use your Venn Diagram and a separate piece of paper to write a rough draft paragraph comparing and contrasting the American Revolution and the Civil War.

**Your paragraph should include:**

- a topic sentence clearly stating that you will be comparing and contrasting the American Revolution and the Civil War.
- two supporting sentences describing how the two wars were alike.
  **Example:** The American Revolution and the Civil War were both fought in the United States over issues that involved freedom.
- two supporting sentences describing how the two wars were different.
  **Example:** While the Revolutionary War started in Massachusetts, the first shots of the Civil War were fired in South Carolina.
- a closing sentence that "sums up" your paragraph.

Have someone edit your rough draft paragraph before writing your final draft in the space below.

# ☆ ✭ ✩ ✮✭☆ VOCABULARY QUIZ ☆ ✭ ✩ ✮✭☆
## NEW ENGLAND STATES
### PART I

**Directions:** Match the vocabulary word on the left with its definition on the right. Put the letter for the definition on the blank next to the vocabulary word it matches. Use each word and definition only once.

1. _____ abolished

2. _____ wampum

3. _____ agriculture

4. _____ allies

5. _____ vowed

6. _____ united

7. _____ trolley

8. _____ ammunition

9. _____ Bermuda

10. _____ citizens

11. _____ transplanted

12. _____ textile

13. _____ sustains

14. _____ constitution

15. _____ debt

16. _____ elections

A. the largest island in Europe. It includes England, Scotland, and Wales.

B. a term once used to describe the continents of North and South America.

C. planting crops and raising farm animals.

D. keeps going without giving up.

E. a person from England who traveled to America in the 1600s and 1700s in search of religious freedom.

F. very large farms in the South where crops of cotton and tobacco were grown and slave labor was generally used.

G. a huge home.

H. stopped or put an end to.

I. an independent European country bordered by the North Sea, Belgium, and Germany.

J. businesses that provide a certain product or service.

K. beads made of shells that were once used for money or decoration by Native Americans.

L. strange, unusual, rare.

M. people living in a city, town, state, or country who enjoy the freedom to vote and participate in government decisions.

N. a woven or knit cloth.

O. a plan which outlines the duties of the government and guarantees the rights of the people.

17. _____ seceded ★

18. _____ profitable ☆

19. _____ plantations ★

20. _____ exotic ☆

21. _____ governor ★

22. _____ historians ★

23. _____ independent ★

24. _____ overthrown ☆

25. _____ New World ★

26. _____ industries ★

27. _____ loyal ☆

28. _____ defeated ★

29. _____ mother country ★

30. _____ Netherlands ☆

31. _____ American Revolution ★

32. _____ colonies ☆

33. _____ Puritan ★

34. _____ Great Britain ★

35. _____ dominion ★

36. _____ New England ☆

37. _____ contrast ★

38. _____ mansion ☆

P. groups of people who are ruled by another country.

Q. large territory with one ruler.

R. came together and formed a single unit.

S. money that is owed to someone else.

T. withdrew from the United States and formed a separate nation.

U. conflict between 13 English colonies in North America and their mother country, Great Britain. Also known as the Revolutionary War.

V. an area in the northeast United States that includes the states of Connecticut, Maine, Massachusetts, New Hampshire, Rhode Island, and Vermont.

W. a British colony located in the Atlantic Ocean.

X. original homeland of the English colonists.

Y. a person who is in charge of an area or group.

Z. to show the differences.

AA. bullets and explosive items used in war.

BB. a business that makes money.

CC. not under the control or rule of another.

DD. groups of people who come together to help one another in times of trouble.

EE. selections of leaders by voting for them.

FF. people who study history.

GG. promised.

HH. moved from one place and settled someplace else.

II. won victory over.

JJ. passenger vehicle that runs on railway tracks set in the street.

KK. removed from power.

LL. faithful.

# MAINE

Maine, the Pine Tree State, is the largest of six New England states in the Northeast region of the United States. Maine's nickname comes from its state tree, the White Pine.

Augusta is the capital of Maine. Augusta is located in the south-central part of the state. In 1628, settlers from the Plymouth Colony in Massachusetts settled in Augusta. The settlers chose Augusta because of its location on the Kennebec River, near a thick forest.

The state bird of Maine is the Chickadee. The state flowers are the White Pine Cone and Tassel, and the state tree is the White Pine. Maine's motto is "I Direct."

## MAINE'S POINTS OF INTEREST

Maine has short summers and cold winters, but recreation is still a big part of this state. Most of Maine's 33,215 square miles are covered with thick forests. These forests are home to moose, deer, black bears, beavers, foxes, lynx, and more than 300 **species** of birds. Maine has at least 5,000 rivers and streams, with more than 2,500 lakes and ponds.

Maine is the least **populated** state east of the Mississippi River. Visitors find plenty of room to enjoy Maine's beautiful scenery while hunting, fishing, boating, skiing, or participating in other outdoor sports. Cadillac Mountain is located in Acadia National Park. The Cadillac Mountain measures 1,532 feet and marks the highest point on the Atlantic **Coast** in all of North America.

## MAINE'S FIRST PEOPLE

The first explorers in Maine found the Abnaki (ab•NAH•kee) people living in the area. The Abnaki spoke the Algonquian (al•GONG•kee•in) language and lived along the river valleys of Maine. Abnaki villages were surrounded by fences with sharp points at the top. Inside these fences were dome-shaped houses made of poles and covered with bark or woven mats. The Europeans called these houses wigwams.

**WIGWAM**

## The Abnaki Confederacy

The Abnaki were farmers who **fertilized** their crops of **maize** by placing one or two dead fish in the soil. During the 1600s, the Abnaki were constantly at war with other Native American tribes. Each tribe in the Abnaki **confederacy** had a war chief and a chief to keep order in the village. The fighting and the arrival of English colonists forced many of the Abnaki to move to the French territories of Québec (kwuh•BEK) and New Brunswick in Canada. This territory was known as **New France** at the time.

## Samuel de Champlain (sham•PLANE)

French explorer Samuel de Champlain was known as the Father of New France. He received this nickname because he discovered the Ottawa River, Lake Champlain, Lake Ontario, and Lake Huron. He also established Québec, the first permanent settlement in New France.

From 1603 to 1633, Champlain made 12 **voyages** from New France to the Northeast region. Like many explorers before and after him, Champlain was searching for a water route that connected North America to Asia.

Getting to Asia was important to Champlain and other European explorers. In Asia they could buy jewels, silk, and spices that were not available in Europe.

The only way to get these products was to buy them from Italian traders. The Italian traders purchased the items from Asia, and sold them at a very high price to Europeans. If European explorers found a water route to Asia, they could buy the things they wanted without paying the Italian traders anything. Unfortunately, there was no direct water route connecting North America to Asia.

**Samuel de Champlain**

In 1604, Champlain visited the present-day state of Maine. He explored and named Mount Desert, the largest island along Maine's coast. He discovered that the New England coast was full of beaver furs. Champlain became friendly with the Abnaki people and other Algonquian tribes. He established a profitable fur trading business with Maine's Native Americans.

In 1609, Champlain and his men joined with New England's Algonquian tribes and **raided** the Iroquois (EAR•uh•kwoy) who lived in present-day New York. The Iroquois were trying to take complete control of the fur trade with the Europeans. Armed with **muskets**, Champlain and his friends easily **defeated** the Iroquois. During the raid, Champlain became the first European to reach a body of water that he named Lake Champlain.

## CONTROL OF MAINE

During the 1600s, many settlements were attempted in Maine. These settlements failed because colonists could not stand the **harsh** weather of Maine. England claimed the rights to Maine based on the earlier **explorations** of John and Sebastian Cabot in 1497. Because of Samuel de Champlain's visit, the French believed that Maine belonged to them. Finally, in 1652, after many years of failed settlements and constant conflict, England permanently claimed Maine.

## NATIVE AMERICAN CONFLICTS IN MAINE

In 1691, a new charter was granted to the colonists of the Massachusetts Bay Colony. This charter gave the English colonists of Massachusetts power over the Maine settlements. Colonists from Massachusetts began moving to Maine. The French and their Native American allies did not give up the land easily. During the 1600s and 1700s, Native American wars made life difficult for the English colonists in Maine.

In 1763, the French and their Native American allies were finally defeated during the French and Indian War. The English colonists had **conquered** the French in America and eastern Canada. The English colonists established a local government and began making money by fishing, building ships, and selling lumber cut from Maine's trees.

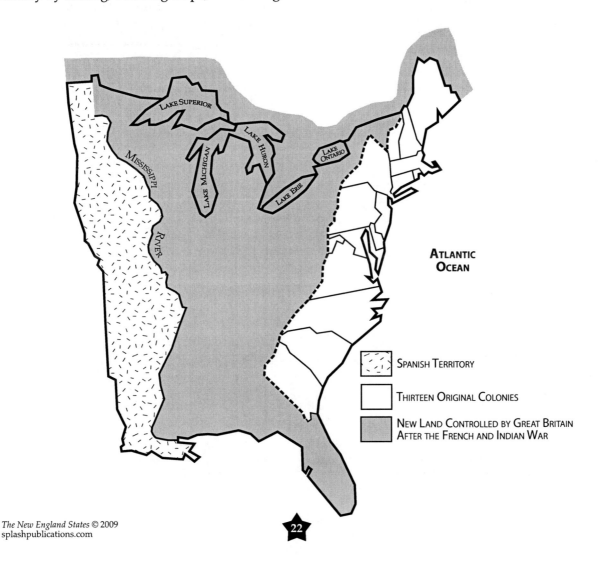

SPANISH TERRITORY

THIRTEEN ORIGINAL COLONIES

NEW LAND CONTROLLED BY GREAT BRITAIN AFTER THE FRENCH AND INDIAN WAR

## ANGRY COLONISTS

Great Britain had sent soldiers and supplies to help England's colonists fight the French and Indian War. After the war was over, Great Britain expected the colonists to pay for the cost of fighting the war. As a result, taxes were placed on everything from sugar to stamps. When the colonists bought these items, they had to pay a tax. The extra money went straight to Great Britain. This angered the colonists.

In 1767, **Parliament** (PAR•luh•ment) passed the Townshend Acts. The Townshend Acts placed a tax on lead, paint, glass, paper, and tea when it was imported into the colonies. The colonists refused to buy any of Great Britain's goods in their stores. This hurt the **merchants** back in Great Britain because the colonists weren't buying any of their imported items.

## THE REVOLUTIONARY WAR

Like the other colonies, Maine refused to buy items that were taxed to raise money for Great Britain. The English colonists in Maine even held their own "tea party" and dumped barrels of British tea into the water.

Maine's soldiers were among the first to fight in the Revolutionary War. Many of the towns along the coast of Maine were attacked by British soldiers during the war. The coastal town of Falmouth was completely destroyed.

In 1775, Benedict Arnold tried unsuccessfully to attack British soldiers in Canada by marching his troops through Maine. Arnold's troops fought hard to force the British soldiers out of Maine, but Great Britain was stronger. Great Britain remained in control of Maine throughout the entire war.

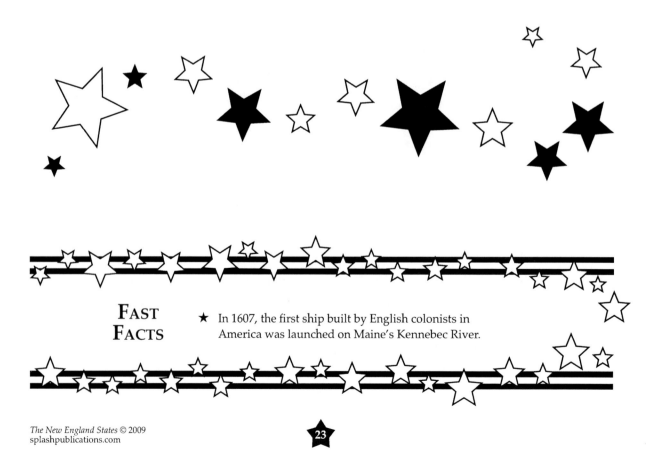

FAST FACTS

★ In 1607, the first ship built by English colonists in America was launched on Maine's Kennebec River.

# THE MISSOURI COMPROMISE

**B**efore the end of the Revolutionary War, the 13 original colonies formed the United States of America. In 1783, the Revolutionary War officially ended. Great Britain and the United States signed a peace treaty. By the time that Maine wanted to became a state, slavery was an angry issue in the United States. There were already 22 states in the Union. Half of them were "free" states that did not permit slavery. The other half were "slave" states that allowed slavery.

Maine wanted to enter the Union as a free state. The slave states were afraid that this would upset the equal balance and give the free states more power. The Missouri **Compromise** finally settled the **debate**. Maine entered the Union as a free state. Missouri entered the Union as a slave state. This kept the United States balanced between free states and slave states. On March 15, 1820, Maine became the 23rd state to join the Union.

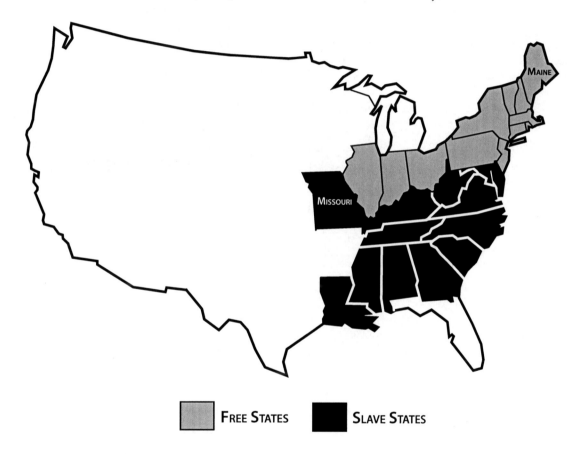

FREE STATES        SLAVE STATES

# THE CIVIL WAR

The population of Maine grew quickly after it became a state. Much of the state's economy was based on ship building and **timber** trade with Asia, Europe, and the **West Indies**. The issue of slavery was decided during the Civil War, when the Northern states fought against the Southern states. As a Northern state, Maine fought to end slavery. Over 73,000 soldiers from Maine served in the Union Army. Almost 7,000 of these men lost their lives. The Northern states were **victorious**. In 1865, the Civil War ended and slavery was abolished.

# MAINE

**Directions:** Read each question. Darken the circle for the correct answer.

**Directions:** Darken the circle for the sentence that uses the underlined word in the same way as the sentence in the box.

1 According to the selection, the first settlers in Maine chose to settle in Augusta because –

   A it was a big area

   B there were no trees in the way

   C it reminded them of England

   D it was located on the Kennebec River, near a thick forest

2 According to the selection, Samuel de Champlain and other explorers were searching for –

   F a water route that connected North America to Asia

   G the Grand Canyon

   H North American animals that they could take back to Europe

   J Native Americans

3 How did the Missouri Compromise keep the free states and slave states balanced?

   A Slavery was no longer permitted in the United States.

   B Maine entered the Union as a free state and Missouri entered the Union as a slave state.

   C Maine and Missouri were not permitted to become states.

   D None of the above.

4 If you wanted to learn more about Maine, you should –

   F draw pictures of the state

   G check out a book from the library about Maine

   H write a letter to Samuel de Champlain

   J travel to Europe

5 | Maine refused to buy British items that were taxed to <u>raise</u> money for Great Britain. |

In which sentence does <u>raise</u> have the same meaning as the sentence above?

   A How much money did we <u>raise</u>?

   B My father received a <u>raise</u> at work.

   C Please <u>raise</u> that window.

   D I <u>raise</u> chickens and cows on my farm.

6 | The Missouri Compromise finally <u>settled</u> the debate. |

In which sentence does <u>settled</u> have the same meaning as the sentence above?

   F We <u>settled</u> the argument.

   G The colonists <u>settled</u> their land.

   H I went swimming after my lunch <u>settled</u>.

   J The chocolate <u>settled</u> at the bottom.

7 | In 1767, Parliament <u>passed</u> the Townshend Acts. |

In which sentence does <u>passed</u> have the same meaning as the sentence above?

   A That car <u>passed</u> us on the highway.

   B I studied hard and <u>passed</u> the test.

   C I spilled milk when you <u>passed</u> the salt.

   D The city <u>passed</u> a law that requires people to walk their dogs on a leash.

**READING**

## Answers

1 Ⓐ Ⓑ Ⓒ Ⓓ     5 Ⓐ Ⓑ Ⓒ Ⓓ

2 Ⓕ Ⓖ Ⓗ Ⓙ     6 Ⓕ Ⓖ Ⓗ Ⓙ

3 Ⓐ Ⓑ Ⓒ Ⓓ     7 Ⓐ Ⓑ Ⓒ Ⓓ

4 Ⓕ Ⓖ Ⓗ Ⓙ

Directions: Read each sentence carefully. Then darken the circle for the correct answer to each question.

Here is a rough draft paragraph about the Abnaki people of Maine. Read the rough draft carefully. Then answer questions 1-4.

---

## THE ABNAKI CONFEDERACY

The Abnaki people were farmers in Maine. They lived along the river
(1)                                              (2)

valleys in Maine. During the 1600s, French explorer Samuel de Champlain
(3)

from France visited Maine and discovered the Abnaki. French settlers soon
(4)

entered Maine and friendly they became with the Abnaki people. The fur
(5)

trade. The French and Abnaki fought and defeated the Iroquois.
(6)

---

**1** Which sentence best combines sentences 1 and 2 without changing their meaning?

  **A** The Abnaki people were farmers in Maine they lived along the river valleys in Maine.

  **B** The Abnaki people were farmers who lived along the river valleys in Maine.

  **C** Along the river valleys in Maine and they were farmers.

  **D** The Abnaki people lived along the river valleys in Maine they were farmers.

**2** Which sentence needlessly repeats a word or group of words?

  **F** 2

  **G** 3

  **H** 5

  **J** 6

**3** Which group of words is <u>not</u> a complete sentence?

  **A** 1

  **B** 3

  **C** 5

  **D** 6

**4** What is the best way to write sentence 4?

  **F** French settlers soon entered Maine and with the Abnaki people they became very friendly.

  **G** French settlers soon entered Maine and became friendly with the Abnaki people.

  **H** The settlers of France entered Maine and the Abnaki people, they became friendly with them.

  **J** As it is written.

LANGUAGE

**Answers**

1 Ⓐ Ⓑ Ⓒ Ⓓ     3 Ⓐ Ⓑ Ⓒ Ⓓ

2 Ⓕ Ⓖ Ⓗ Ⓙ     4 Ⓕ Ⓖ Ⓗ Ⓙ

the source

**T**hink about the resources we use to learn about history. Reading books, seeing movies, looking at photographs, studying maps, searching the Internet, digging for bones, and holding pieces of pottery are some of the ways that we learn about the past.

There are two types of sources to help us learn about what happened in the past. Primary sources are recorded by people who were there at the time. If you have ever read a diary or an **autobiography**, then you were reading something that was written by the person who was actually recording the events and experiences as they were happening. Diaries and autobiographies are primary sources. Letters, interviews, photographs, original maps, bones, and pieces of pottery are other examples of primary sources because they give us "first-hand" knowledge of an event that took place in history.

Secondary sources are recorded by people after an event took place. Many books have been written about important historical events and people. A book written in 1998 about the life of French explorer Samuel de Champlain is a secondary source because the author wasn't actually there to interview the famous explorer and can't give any "first-hand" knowledge. Movies, **biographies,** newspaper stories, and encyclopedias are other examples of secondary sources because they give us "second-hand" knowledge of events that took place in history.

**Y**ou have just finished studying about Connecticut and Maine. The people and events from these two states helped shape American history.

**I**n this activity, you will decide whether a source of information is a primary source or a secondary source. On the lines provided, put a "P" next to the primary sources and an "S" next to the secondary sources.

1. _____ A photograph of an American Robin, Connecticut's state bird.

2. _____ The bible that Thomas Hooker carried from Massachusetts to Connecticut.

3. _____ An encyclopedia article written about the Pequot War.

4. _____ The taped recording of Nathan Hale speaking his last words before he was hanged.

5. _____ A painting of Maine's "tea party," showing colonists dumping tea into the water.

6. _____ The original map of the Missouri Compromise.

7. _____ Harriet Beecher Stowe's biography.

# ☆ ✦ ✧ ✦ ✦ ✧ VOCABULARY QUIZ ☆ ✦ ✧ ✦ ✦ ✧
## NEW ENGLAND STATES
## PART II

**Directions:** Match the vocabulary word on the left with its definition on the right. Put the letter for the definition on the blank next to the vocabulary word it matches. Use each word and definition only once.

1. _____ accused

2. _____ adopted

3. _____ West Indies

4. _____ voyages

5. _____ antislavery

6. _____ appointed

7. _____ borders

8. _____ capital

9. _____ species

10. _____ New France

11. _____ charter

12. _____ colonists

13. _____ maize

14. _____ mammals

15. _____ conquered

A. lies right next to something.

B. one of seven continents in the world. Bounded by Alaska in the northwest, Greenland in the northeast, Florida in the southeast, and Mexico in the southwest.

C. the number of people living in a place.

D. a chain of about 1,000 islands in the Caribbean Sea that stretches from the southern tip of Florida to the northeastern corner of South America.

E. groups of plants or animals that are alike in many ways.

F. a region located on the southern part of the island of Great Britain.

G. chosen or selected.

H. five large lakes located in North America at the border between Canada and the United States. The names of the lakes are Superior, Michigan, Huron, Erie, and Ontario.

I. a formal agreement.

J. the nation formed by the Southern states during the Civil War.

K. a short phrase describing conduct or principles.

L. lived or settled in a place.

M. against slavery.

N. gave up completely.

16. _____ coast

17. _____ Continental Army

18. _____ treaty

19. _____ territories

20. _____ surrendered

21. _____ North America

22. _____ manufacturing

23. _____ motto

24. _____ island

25. _____ inhabited

26. _____ imported

27. _____ Great Lakes

28. _____ Europeans

29. _____ economy

30. _____ England

31. _____ victorious

32. _____ compromise

33. _____ muskets

34. _____ populated

35. _____ conflict

36. _____ Confederate States of America

O. American troops that fought against Great Britain during the Revolutionary War.

P. an agreement reached when each side changes or gives up some of its demands.

Q. accepted and put into action.

R. an area of land that borders water.

S. people who come from the continent of Europe.

T. Native American corn.

U. having won a victory.

V. defeated by force.

W. making something from raw materials by hand or machinery.

X. the city that serves as the center of government for the state.

Y. brought items into a country for the purpose of selling them.

Z. journeys that are usually made by water.

AA. a contract which gives one group power over another.

BB. guns that are loaded through the muzzle.

CC. blamed or charged with a crime.

DD. people who live in a colony.

EE. areas of land controlled by a person or group of people.

FF. the way a city, state, or country makes money.

GG. land surrounded on all sides by water.

HH. the part of North America claimed by France from the early 1600s until 1763.

II. warm-blooded animals who feed their young with milk, have backbones, and are covered with hair.

JJ. a struggle or disagreement.

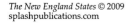

# MASSACHUSETTS

**M**assachusetts, the Bay State, is one of six New England states located in the Northeast region of the United States. Massachusetts was one of the 13 original states in America. It was also home to two of the 13 original colonies, Plymouth and the Massachusetts Bay colony. It is nicknamed the Bay State because of an early settlement on Cape Cod Bay.

The capital of Massachusetts is Boston, the largest city in all of New England. Boston is the Northeast region's most important **seaport**. Those who visit Boston on December 16th of each year can see a **reenactment** of the Boston Tea Party in the Boston **Harbor**.

The state bird of Massachusetts is the Chickadee. The state flower is the Mayflower, and the state tree is the American Elm. The state motto of Massachusetts is "By the Sword We Seek Peace, but Peace Only Under **Liberty**."

## POINTS OF INTEREST IN MASSACHUSETTS

The name Massachusetts comes from Native American words that mean "near the great mountain." Historians believe that the great mountain is the tallest point of the Blue Hills, a recreation area in Massachusetts.

Visitors to Massachusetts enjoy both land and water. Forests cover more than three million acres of the state. Berkshire Hills is a favorite place in Massachusetts for summer camping and winter snow skiing. The famous **resort** area known as Cape Cod is located on the elbow-shaped eastern **peninsula** of the state. Fishing, boating, and swimming are popular activities on Cape Cod. The islands of Nantucket and Martha's Vinyard are also part of Massachusetts.

Of course, like all of the New England states, history is **preserved** in the many historic villages, buildings, **monuments**, museums, and libraries in Massachusetts. There are over 150 national historic sites in Massachusetts. The Pilgrim National Wax Museum in Plymouth is the only wax museum in the United States that is completely **devoted** to the story of the **Pilgrims**.

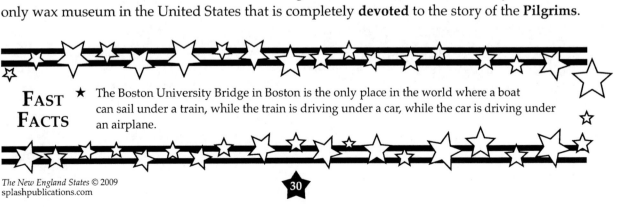

**FAST FACTS** ★ The Boston University Bridge in Boston is the only place in the world where a boat can sail under a train, while the train is driving under a car, while the car is driving under an airplane.

## The First People in Massachusetts

Long before the Europeans settled in Massachusetts, Native Americans lived there. The largest group of Native Americans in Massachusetts was a confederacy that included the Massachuset, Nauset (NAW•set), Nipmuc (NIP•muck), and Wampanoag (wam•puh•NO•ag) tribes. They spoke the Algonquian (al•GONG•kee•in) language and settled in permanent villages along the rivers in Massachusetts. The confederacy also settled in the present-day city of Boston. These Native Americans hunted, fished, and grew crops of corn, beans, and squash.

In 1498, John Cabot became the first explorer to sail along the coast of Massachusetts. Cabot was an Italian who explored North America for England. He was looking for a water route to Asia. Many other explorers also sailed around the New England coast. None of them stayed in Massachusetts or established any permanent settlements. This pleased the Native Americans who were not eager to give up their land in Massachusetts to white settlers.

## The Pilgrims Land in Massachusetts

The first European settlers in all of New England were the Pilgrims. On September 6, 1620, the Pilgrims left England and sailed for Virginia on *The Mayflower*. Stormy weather took them off course. They landed in Massachusetts Bay instead of Virginia. Before leaving their ship, the men wrote and signed the Mayflower Compact. The Mayflower Compact established rules and laws for the settlers to obey.

The Pilgrims named their new colony Plymouth. This was in honor of the city in England from which they had come. They elected John Carver as the governor of their colony. Unfortunately, the Pilgrims were completely unprepared for **survival** in Massachusetts. During their first winter, almost half of the Pilgrims died.

The next spring, with the help of a Native American named Squanto, the Pilgrims learned to fish, hunt, and grow corn. The Pilgrims signed a peace treaty with the Native Americans. In the fall of 1621, the Pilgrims and the Native Americans celebrated the first Thanksgiving.

**The Mayflower**

# THE MASSACHUSETTS BAY COMPANY

Other settlers traveled from England to establish colonies in Massachusetts. In 1629, King Charles I of England allowed a group of wealthy businessmen to start a colony between the Charles River and the Merrimack River in Massachusetts. They called themselves the Massachusetts Bay Company.

The Massachusetts Bay Company planned to make money by setting up the first trading business in North America. The businessmen also wanted to grant religious freedom to its settlers. During the next 13 years, more than 20,000 Puritans traveled to New England in search of religious freedom.

# THE KING PHILIP'S WAR

As the colonies grew, there were more white settlers than Native Americans. The Native Americans feared they would be forced from their land.

In 1675, the Native Americans started the King Philip's War to drive out the English settlers. King Philip, chief of the Wampanoag tribe, led his people in several battles that destroyed many English settlements in Massachusetts.

Though the Native Americans were successful in many of the battles, the English colonists were stronger. The Native Americans were defeated.

# THE BOSTON MASSACRE

Massachusetts was the center of activity at the beginning of the American Revolution. The colonists showed their anger toward Great Britain's unfair taxes.

In 1770, British troops were sent to Boston to keep peace. The colonists threw rocks and eggs at the soldiers. At one point the British soldiers fired into the crowd and killed five colonists. They were the first colonists to lose their lives in **protest** against Great Britain's rules.

**BRITISH SOLDIER**

The killing of the five colonists became known as the Boston **Massacre**. After the Boston Massacre, Great Britain removed the troops from Boston and ended all of the taxes except for the tax on tea.

## The Boston Tea Party

The colonists responded to the Boston Massacre and the tea tax by **boycotting** British tea. Great Britain even tried to trick the colonists into buying tea by lowering the price of it and then adding the tax. On December 16, 1773, three ships from Great Britain entered the Boston Harbor loaded with tea. A group of colonists led by Samuel Adams **disguised** themselves as Native Americans. They raided the British ships and dumped 342 chests of British tea into the Boston Harbor. The event, known as the Boston Tea Party, angered King George III of England. He immediately passed laws to punish the colonists for this act.

## The Intolerable Acts

The laws passed by Great Britain became known as the **Intolerable** Acts. One law closed the Boston Harbor until the colonists agreed to pay for the lost tea and show proper respect for Great Britain's authority. Another law changed the Massachusetts charter of 1691. It took away the right of the colonists to govern themselves. Great Britain also sent the British troops back to Boston. The colonists were once again required to provide housing and food for the British soldiers.

The Intolerable Acts created even more **hostility** and anger toward Great Britain. The colonists refused to give in to these demands. If they obeyed Great Britain, the colonists gave up the freedom for which they had worked so hard. The colonists had risked everything to come to America where they could live freely. Now they faced the possibility of being ruled by a country 3,000 miles away.

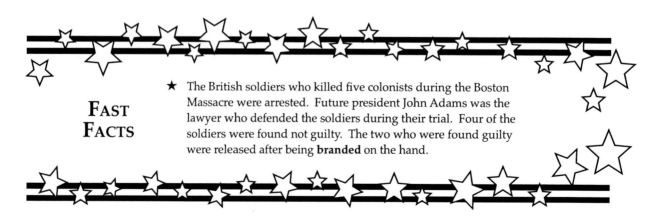

**Fast Facts**

★ The British soldiers who killed five colonists during the Boston Massacre were arrested. Future president John Adams was the lawyer who defended the soldiers during their trial. Four of the soldiers were found not guilty. The two who were found guilty were released after being **branded** on the hand.

# THE FIRST CONTINENTAL CONGRESS

In September, 1774, every colony, except Georgia, sent **representatives** to the First **Continental Congress** in Philadelphia. The reason for the meeting was to decide what to do about Great Britain's cruel treatment of the colonists. The leaders of the meeting included Samuel Adams and John Adams of Massachusetts, George Washington and Patrick Henry of Virginia, and Benjamin Franklin of Pennsylvania.

The colonists were angry with Great Britain's unfair taxes and the Intolerable Acts. Britain made it clear that it was not going to loosen its grip on the colonies. The representatives voted to end all trade with Great Britain until the Intolerable Acts were **repealed**. They also wrote letters to King George III asking him to abolish the Acts. The **delegates** of the Continental Congress told the colonists to begin training for war.

The colonists prepared for war. They had never formally organized an army or navy, but white men from 16 to 60 years old volunteered to form a **militia** (muh•LIH•shuh). Groups of **minutemen** also prepared themselves for battle. Weapons and gunpowder were gathered and stored in the village of Concord, Massachusetts. British spies found out about the weapons and planned a surprise raid to capture the weapons and take them away. Great Britain hoped that taking away the colonists' weapons would avoid a war.

# PAUL REVERE'S FAMOUS RIDE

Just after midnight on April 18, 1775, seven hundred British soldiers dressed in bright red coats left Boston. They marched toward the village of Concord. Paul Revere, a silversmith, and his friend William Dawes, were watching. They rode on horseback to warn the colonists that the British Redcoats were coming. Paul Revere's warning gave the colonists in Concord enough time to hide most of their weapons and gunpowder before the British soldiers arrived.

# THE BATTLES OF LEXINGTON AND CONCORD

Minutemen who heard Paul Revere's warning met the British soldiers in the town of Lexington, Massachusetts. The minutemen tried to keep the Redcoats from entering the village of Concord. The first shots of the Revolutionary War were fired in Lexington. Several minutemen were killed or wounded.

The British troops continued on to Concord where they searched for the hidden weapons. Again, they were met by a group of minutemen who had been warned that the Redcoats were coming. In a brief battle, three Redcoats and two minutemen were killed.

PAUL REVERE

The British soldiers turned back to Boston. Along the way, more minutemen fired at them from behind trees and stone fences. Over 200 British Redcoats and 90 American minutemen were wounded and killed during the battle.

## THE BATTLE OF BUNKER HILL

On June 17, 1775, the first major battle of the American Revolution was fought. It is often called the Battle of Bunker Hill, but the fighting actually broke out on Breed's Hill. Massachusetts is surrounded by huge hills that overlook the city of Boston. Both British and American troops planned to take control of these hills. The Americans reached the top of Breed's Hill first. British troops led by General William Howe attacked the Americans in an effort to take over the hill.

The American troops put up a good fight, but they ran out of gunpowder and were forced to **flee**. More than 1,000 British soldiers and 400 American soldiers were killed or wounded during the bloodiest battle of the entire Revolutionary War. Even though the Americans did not win the battle, they made it clear to Great Britain that they were prepared to fight.

## MASSACHUSETTS BECOMES A STATE

Fighting in Massachusetts ended with the battle of Bunker Hill. In 1776, the city of Boston was **evacuated**. In 1780, one year before the colonists declared victory in the Revolutionary War, the people of Massachusetts made a bold stand for independence when they adopted a state constitution. John Hancock was elected as the first governor of Massachusetts. Eight years later, on February 6, 1788, Massachusetts become the sixth state to join the Union.

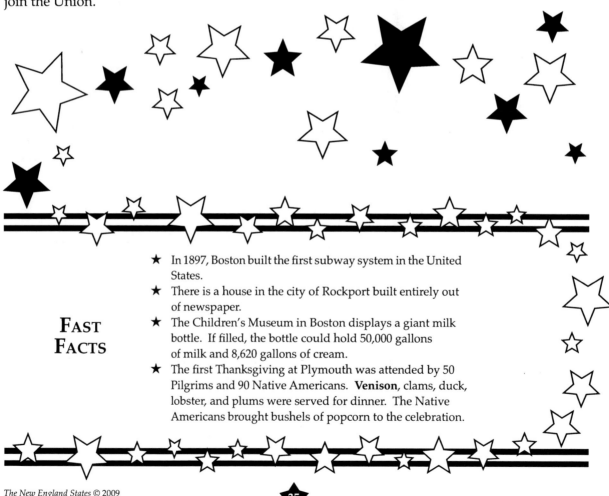

**FAST FACTS**

★ In 1897, Boston built the first subway system in the United States.
★ There is a house in the city of Rockport built entirely out of newspaper.
★ The Children's Museum in Boston displays a giant milk bottle. If filled, the bottle could hold 50,000 gallons of milk and 8,620 gallons of cream.
★ The first Thanksgiving at Plymouth was attended by 50 Pilgrims and 90 Native Americans. **Venison**, clams, duck, lobster, and plums were served for dinner. The Native Americans brought bushels of popcorn to the celebration.

# THE ECONOMY IN MASSACHUSETTS

As a state, Massachusetts developed into a major manufacturing center. Textile factories were built throughout Massachusetts. In 1825, the Erie **Canal** opened. Massachusetts used the canal to send the products from its factories to places in the western part of the United States. A few years later, Elias Howe invented the sewing machine. This machine helped the textile and shoe factories produce more products in less time.

Most of the people who lived in the Southern states owned slaves to help them run their large plantations and farms. There were very few large farms in Massachusetts, so very few people in Massachusetts owned slaves. In fact, many people in Massachusetts wanted to see slavery abolished. They helped runaway slaves escape from the South.

**PHILLIS WHEATLEY**

## PHILLIS WHEATLEY

Phillis Wheatley was brought to Boston on a slave ship from Africa when she was just eight years old. John Wheatley, a wealthy merchant, bought Phillis as a servant for his wife. The Wheatleys gave Phillis their last name. They taught her how to read and write. Phillis also studied **geography**, history, and Latin. Educating a slave was against the law in most colonies.

Phillis began to write poetry when she was about 14 years old. She wrote about religion, slavery, and the colonists' fight for independence. In her poems she compared her life as a slave to the colonists' desire for independence from Great Britain.

The Wheatleys took Phillis to England where some of her poems were published. After returning from England, the Wheatleys gave Phillis her freedom. She became known as America's first important African American poet.

## THE CIVIL WAR

In 1861, the Civil War broke out between the Northern states and the Southern states. The United States had fallen apart over the issue of slavery.

Massachusetts was the first state to send troops to help put an end to slavery and bring the United States back together. It was also the first state to form troops of black soldiers.

More than 146,000 men from Massachusetts fought during the Civil War. When the Civil War ended, the Northern states had been successful. Slavery was abolished and the United States joined back together as one Union.

Name _____

Directions: Read each question. Darken the circle for the correct answer.

Directions: Darken the circle for the word or words that give the meaning of the underlined word.

1 According to the information about Massachusetts, who were the first Europeans to settle in all of New England?

   A Russians

   B Pilgrims

   C Spanish

   D British soldiers

2 During the Boston Tea Party, what did the colonists do before dumping English tea into the Boston Harbor?

   F They threw rocks at the British ships.

   G They killed five British soldiers.

   H They disguised themselves as Native Americans.

   J They promised to obey Great Britain's laws.

3 The boxes below show events from the Revolutionary War.

| Paul Revere warned the colonists that the British were coming. | | The Americans lost the Battle of Bunker Hill. |
|---|---|---|
| 1 | 2 | 3 |

Which event belongs in the second box?

   A Massachusetts became a state.

   B The Native Americans were defeated during King Philip's War.

   C Five colonists were killed during the Boston Massacre.

   D The first shots of the Revolutionary War were fired in the town of Lexington.

4 The history of Massachusetts is preserved in many historic buildings throughout the state. Preserved means –

   F thrown away

   G eaten

   H returned

   J saved

5 The colonists in Massachusetts were the first to lose their lives in protest against Great Britain's rules. Protest means –

   A argue against

   B agree with

   C tell the truth

   D find something

6 They voted to end all trade with Great Britain until the Intolerable Acts were repealed. Repealed means –

   F saved

   G bought

   H removed

   J sold

7 In 1776, the city of Boston was evacuated. Evacuated means –

   A fought against the enemy

   B died from sickness or disease

   C ordered not to do something

   D removed people from a place of danger

READING

Answers

1 Ⓐ Ⓑ Ⓒ Ⓓ    5 Ⓐ Ⓑ Ⓒ Ⓓ
2 Ⓕ Ⓖ Ⓗ Ⓙ    6 Ⓕ Ⓖ Ⓗ Ⓙ
3 Ⓐ Ⓑ Ⓒ Ⓓ    7 Ⓐ Ⓑ Ⓒ Ⓓ
4 Ⓕ Ⓖ Ⓗ Ⓙ

**Directions: Read each sentence carefully. Then darken the circle for the correct answer to each question.**

Here is a rough draft paragraph about Paul Revere. There are certain words and phrases underlined. Read the rough draft carefully. Then answer questions 1-5.

---

## PAUL REVERE

(1) Paul Revere was born on January 1, 1735. (2) <u>He lives in Boston,</u> Massachusetts and worked as a silversmith. (3) Paul Revere supported the <u>colonists' independence</u> from Great Britain. (4) He was involved in the Boston Massacre and used his skills as a silversmith <u>too make cannonballs</u> for the Revolutionary War. (5) Revere was 40 years old when he became <u>a American hero.</u> (6) He rode on horseback from Boston to Concord and warned the colonists that the <u>British was coming.</u>

---

**1** **In sentence 2, <u>He lives in Boston</u> is best written –**

   **A** He is living in Boston

   **B** He wants to live in Boston

   **C** He lived in Boston

   **D** As it is written.

**2** **In sentence 3, <u>colonists' independence</u> is best written –**

   **F** colonists independence

   **G** colonist's independence

   **H** colonist independence

   **J** As it is written.

**3** **In sentence 4, <u>too make cannonballs</u> is best written –**

   **A** two make cannonballs

   **B** tow make cannonballs

   **C** to make cannonballs

   **D** As it is written.

**4** **In sentence 5, <u>a American hero</u> is best written –**

   **F** an American hero

   **G** a America hero

   **H** an America's hero

   **J** As it is written.

**5** **In sentence 6, <u>British was coming</u> is best written –**

   **A** British is coming

   **B** British are coming

   **C** British were coming

   **D** As it is written.

---

**LANGUAGE**

**Answers**

1 Ⓐ Ⓑ Ⓒ Ⓓ    4 Ⓕ Ⓖ Ⓗ Ⓙ

2 Ⓕ Ⓖ Ⓗ Ⓙ    5 Ⓐ Ⓑ Ⓒ Ⓓ

3 Ⓐ Ⓑ Ⓒ Ⓓ

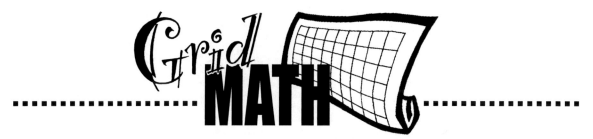

**Grid Math** is a fun way to learn an important skill. Grids are used to find places on maps, to track weather patterns, and in space exploration.

**For Example:** If you want to locate a place where 2 meets 3 (2,3), you would go **over** to 2 and **up** to 3. On a map or an atlas, (2,3) may be the place where you would find the name of your city.

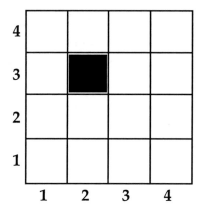

**Directions:** In this activity you will use a grid system to put together a puzzle that should remind you of an important event in the history of Massachusetts. You will need the 48 puzzle pieces (some of the puzzle pieces are below and the rest of them are on the next page), and the blank grid.

1. Cut out the puzzle pieces **one at a time** (cut around the thick black line of the square). Glue **that** piece in its proper place on the empty grid before cutting out the next piece. Make sure that you do not turn the puzzle piece upside down or turn it on its side before gluing it; the way it looks before you cut it out is the way it should be glued onto the grid.

2. Follow the example above: If the puzzle piece is labeled (4,1), glue that piece in the space where 4 meets 1 on the grid by going <u>over</u> to 4 and <u>up</u> to 1. **(4,1)** has been done for you as an example.

3. When you are finished, color in your picture with your coloring pencils.

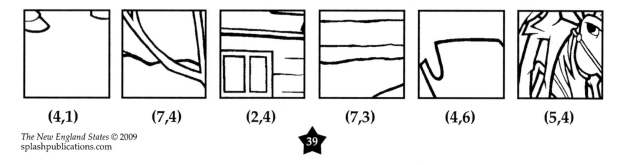

(4,1)      (7,4)      (2,4)      (7,3)      (4,6)      (5,4)

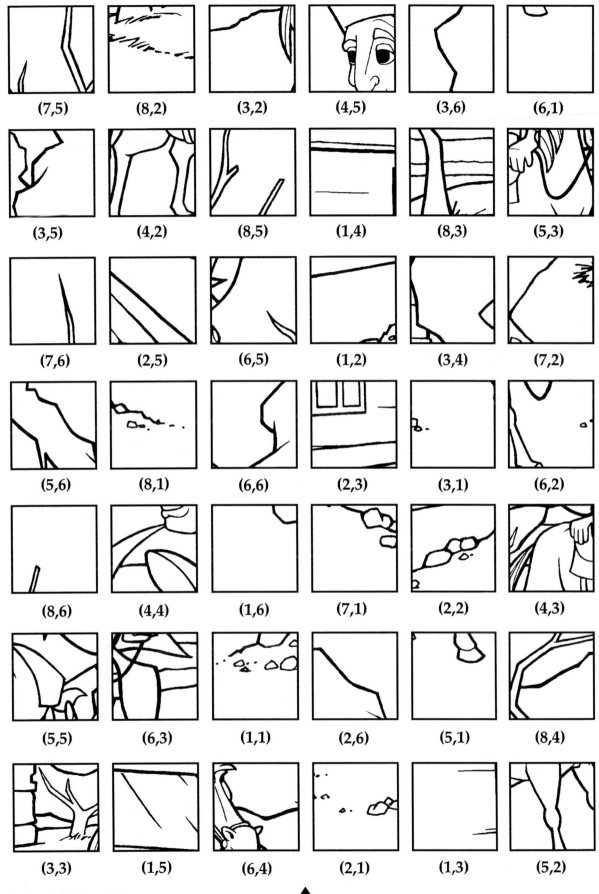

(7,5)  (8,2)  (3,2)  (4,5)  (3,6)  (6,1)

(3,5)  (4,2)  (8,5)  (1,4)  (8,3)  (5,3)

(7,6)  (2,5)  (6,5)  (1,2)  (3,4)  (7,2)

(5,6)  (8,1)  (6,6)  (2,3)  (3,1)  (6,2)

(8,6)  (4,4)  (1,6)  (7,1)  (2,2)  (4,3)

(5,5)  (6,3)  (1,1)  (2,6)  (5,1)  (8,4)

(3,3)  (1,5)  (6,4)  (2,1)  (1,3)  (5,2)

NAME _____

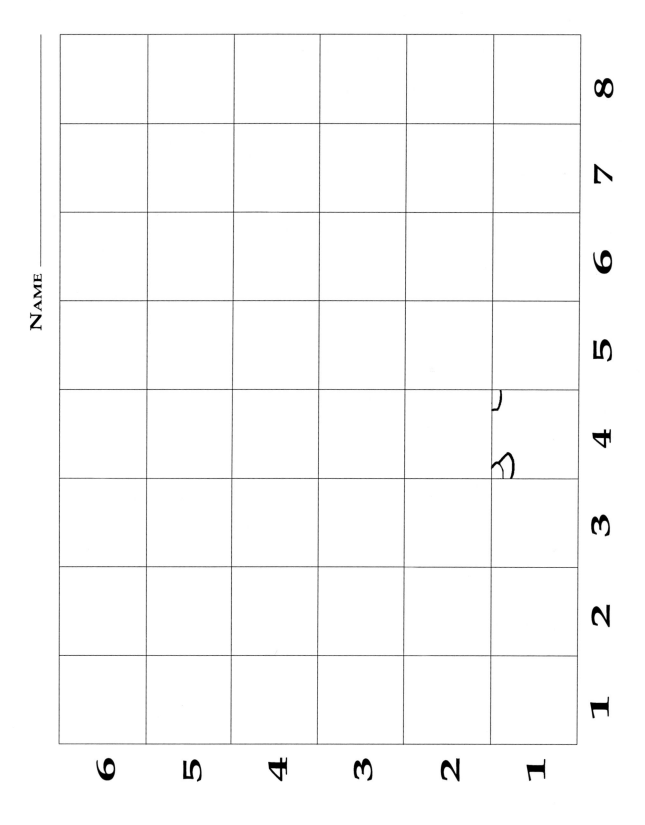

1 2 3 4 5 6 7 8

6 5 4 3 2 1

*The New England States* © 2009
splashpublications.com

# ☆ ✦ ☆ ★✦☆ VOCABULARY QUIZ ☆ ✦ ☆ ★✦☆
## NEW ENGLAND STATES
### PART III

**Directions:**   Match the vocabulary word on the left with its definition on the right.  Put the letter for the definition on the blank next to the vocabulary word it matches.  Use each word and definition only once.

1. _____ debate

2. _____ fertilized

3. _____ merchants

4. _____ venison

5. _____ Parliament

6. _____ explorations

7. _____ autobiography

8. _____ seaport

9. _____ boycotting

10. _____ branded

11. _____ canal

12. _____ resort

13. _____ delegates

14. _____ devoted

15. _____ disguised

16. _____ hostility

A.  a place where people go for a vacation.

B.  changed appearance to keep from being recognized.

C.  deer meat.

D.  attacked suddenly.

E.  a port, harbor, or town within reach of seagoing ships.

F.  to argue against something believed to be unfair.

G.  continuing to live.

H.  the violent and cruel killing of a large number of people.

I.  burned a mark into the skin of a person or animal.  During the early days of history, this was used for criminals to easily identify them as law breakers.

J.  done away with; removed.

K.  added a material to the soil to make crops grow better.

L.  buildings, stones, or statues created to remember a person or event.

M.  trips taken for the purpose of discovering something.

N.  to run away from danger.

O.  the group of leaders from the 13 original colonies who had the power to make laws and decisions for the newly formed United States.

17. _____ representatives

18. _____ repealed

19. _____ reenactment

20. _____ raided

21. _____ evacuated

22. _____ Continental Congress

23. _____ intolerable

24. _____ protest

25. _____ preserved

26. _____ liberty

27. _____ massacre

28. _____ Pilgrims

29. _____ peninsula

30. _____ monuments

31. _____ minutemen

32. _____ militia

33. _____ harsh

34. _____ harbor

35. _____ flee

36. _____ biographies

37. _____ survival

38. _____ geography

P.  the story of your life written by you.

Q.  very uncomfortable conditions.

R.  people sent with power to represent others.

S.  protected from injury or ruin so more can be learned.

T.  buyers and sellers who do so for profit.

U.  a group of men having some military training who are called upon only in emergencies.

V.  promised to be loyal to something.

W.  the English colonists who founded the first permanent settlement in New England at Plymouth in 1620.

X.  the group of people in Great Britain that makes the laws.

Y.  the study of the Earth.

Z.  a piece of land extending into a body of water.

AA. a man-made waterway for boats or for watering crops.

BB. a sheltered area of water deep enough to provide ships a place to anchor.

CC. freedom to do as one pleases.

DD. a discussion that gives arguments for and against a subject.

EE. removed people from a place of danger.

FF. people chosen to speak or act for an entire group.

GG. unbearable.

HH. anger.

II.  refusing to buy.

JJ.  to act or perform again.

KK. stories of a person's life written by someone else.

LL. groups of armed men who were prepared to fight on a minute's notice during the Revolutionary War.

# NEW HAMPSHIRE

New Hampshire, the **Granite** State, is one of six New England states in the Northeast region of the United States. New Hampshire is one of the smallest states in the Union. It takes up an area of less than 10,000 square miles. New Hampshire's nickname comes from the fact that the state contains so many granite **formations** and deposits.

The capital of New Hampshire is Concord. Concord lies on the west bank of the Merrimack River. The capital city's major industry is printing. It also manufactures electronic equipment, leather, wood, and metal products.

The state bird of New Hampshire is the Purple Finch. The state flower is the Purple Lilac, and the state tree is the White Birch. New Hampshire's motto is "Live Free or Die."

## NEW HAMPSHIRE'S POINTS OF INTEREST

New Hampshire's visitors enjoy camping, hiking, or skiing in the White Mountains. The 86 peaks of the White Mountains are part of the largest mountain range in the northeastern United States.

One of the most famous sights of the White Mountains is the "Old Man of the Mountain." This rock formation on Profile Mountain looks like a human face. The White Mountains also feature the **glacial** (GLAY•shul) caverns of Lost River. Visitors to Mount Washington enjoy the view from the top of New England's highest mountain.

Eighty-five percent of New Hampshire is covered with woods. These woods are home to deer, black bear, moose, bobcat, and several smaller mammals. There are over 1,300 lakes and ponds in New Hampshire. The larger lakes have well-developed resorts with excellent boating and fishing facilities. The southeastern corner of New Hampshire dips into the Atlantic Ocean. Visitors to the coastline enjoy 18 miles of sandy beaches. Hampton Beach is New Hampshire's most popular seaside resort.

Throughout New Hampshire are homes from the 1700s. These historic homes preserve New Hampshire's history. Some of the historic sites include the Franklin Pierce Homestead, the birthplace of Daniel Webster, and the Robert Frost Farm. New Hampshire also features 53 covered bridges dating back to the 1800s.

# NEW HAMPSHIRE'S FIRST PEOPLE

More than 12,000 Native Americans who spoke the Algonquian (al•GONG•kee•in) language inhabited New Hampshire before the arrival of European explorers. About half of these people belonged to the Pennacook tribe. The Pennacook lived in the Merrimack River Valley of New Hampshire. They were farmers who lived in permanent villages. The Pennacook also hunted during the year. During the summer some members of the tribe traveled to the seacoast for fishing and gathering shellfish.

In 1603, the first recorded visit to New Hampshire was made. English sea captain Martin Pring explored the shoreline and a small area of New Hampshire's **interior**. Pring was hired by some wealthy merchants in England to travel to America. He was instructed to find a shortcut to Asia. The wealthy businessmen also wanted Pring to bring back American plants and roots that could cure colds and other illnesses. Pring did not find the plants or the easy route to Asia. He did find an area that was full of forests and fur-bearing animals.

Pring was not interested in establishing any permanent settlements in New Hampshire. In 1605, French explorer Samuel de Champlain (sham•PLANE) visited New Hampshire. Like Pring, Champlain was also searching for a water route to Asia. Champlain made maps of the New England coastline for France.

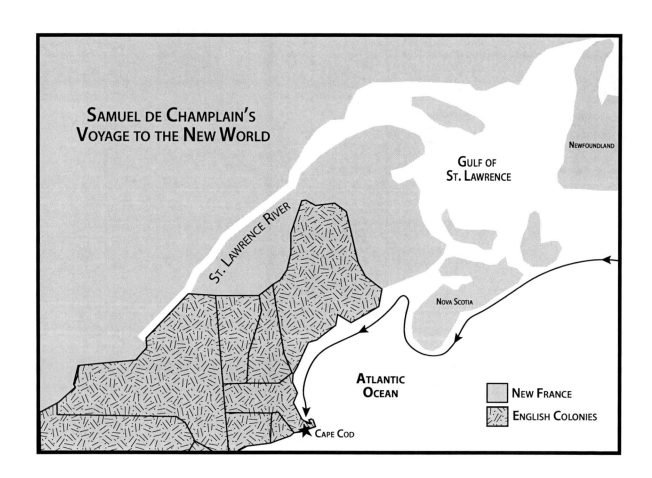

# JOHN SMITH

English explorer John Smith had already helped establish England's first American colony in Jamestown, Virginia. He had been hired by wealthy businessmen in London to establish Jamestown.

In 1609, Smith was badly injured in a gunpowder explosion. He left Virginia and returned to England for medical care.

In 1614, John Smith got the chance to return to America. He was hired to lead an English whale-hunting, fishing, and fur-trading **expedition** to what is now the northeastern United States.

On this trip to America, Smith explored the coast of New Hampshire. He made notes about the land, people, plants, and animals.

John Smith named the area he visited New England. He drew the first good maps of the New England area.

John Smith returned to England and wrote books about his adventures in America. He encouraged other English colonists to travel to America. He warned them that it would take a lot of hard work and determination to settle in America.

**JOHN SMITH**

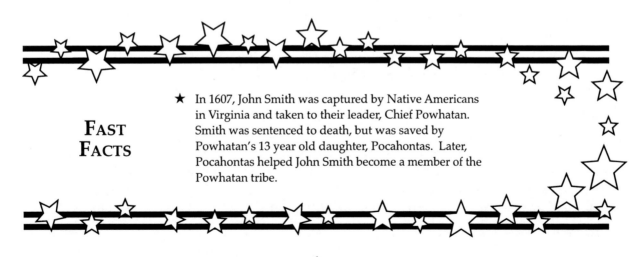

**FAST FACTS**

★ In 1607, John Smith was captured by Native Americans in Virginia and taken to their leader, Chief Powhatan. Smith was sentenced to death, but was saved by Powhatan's 13 year old daughter, Pocahontas. Later, Pocahontas helped John Smith become a member of the Powhatan tribe.

# SETTLEMENTS IN NEW HAMPSHIRE

In 1623, New Hampshire's first permanent settlements were **founded.** A few settlers arrived from Scotland. They established farms, fishing operations, and a trading post in the present-day town of Rye located on the Atlantic Coast. Settlers from London arrived a few years later and made a settlement north of Rye in Dover. By 1638, other settlements had been established in the present-day cities of Portsmouth, Exeter, and Hampton.

The Native Americans were friendly to the Europeans and even taught them many survival skills. With the help of the Native Americans, the European settlers learned how to grow corn, tap maple trees for syrup, and make canoes. The Native Americans also taught the settlers where to find the best hunting places. In return, the Europeans gave the Native Americans metal tools, blankets, and weapons. The weapons were valuable for hunting and protection from enemy tribes.

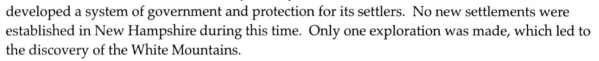

From the early 1640s until 1679, the New Hampshire towns were under the leadership of the Massachusetts Bay Colony. This group had already established a colony in Massachusetts. The Massachusetts Bay Colony developed a system of government and protection for its settlers. No new settlements were established in New Hampshire during this time. Only one exploration was made, which led to the discovery of the White Mountains.

# A ROYAL COLONY

In 1680, New Hampshire became a royal colony. The King of England selected a president and a **council** for the colony. Conflicts arose between New Hampshire and Massachusetts over land **boundaries.** The leaders of the Massachusetts Bay Colony gave land in New Hampshire to its settlers. The settlers in New Hampshire claimed that this land belonged to them. The New Hampshire settlers felt that the Massachusetts Bay Colony had no right to give it away.

In 1686, King James II took away the colonists' right to make their own laws and rules. He angered the New England colonists when he joined New Hampshire, Massachusetts, Rhode Island, Connecticut, New Jersey, and New York into a single **province.** He named the province the Dominion of New England. King James II appointed Sir Edmund Andros governor of the province.

Sir Edmund Andros was a mean governor. He taxed the colonists of the province and used the money to become wealthy. Anyone who refused to pay the taxes was sent to jail. In the spring of 1689, the colonists captured Governor Andros and threw him in jail. Andros was sent back to England. The New England colonists took charge of the province and once again started making their own laws and rules.

# NATIVE AMERICAN CONFLICTS IN NEW HAMPSHIRE

Other New England colonies were constantly at war with the Native Americans. The settlers in New Hampshire maintained peaceful relationships with the Native peoples. This changed as the population of New Hampshire grew. New Hampshire's settlers took control of Native American hunting and fishing territories. The new settlers brought **livestock** with them. The livestock grazed on the crops in the Native Americans' fields. This angered the Native Americans.

The English settlers wanted control of the land in New Hampshire. The French wanted control of New Hampshire's hunting territories. The Native Americans in New Hampshire were already angry with the English settlers. Many of the tribes sided with the French. Together they fought to drive the English colonists from New Hampshire.

## THE KING WILLIAM'S WAR

The most **destructive** battle of this period was the King William's War. Beginning in 1689, Native Americans attacked white settlements, burned houses, killed hundreds of settlers, and took many of the settlers **captive**. The women and children were marched into Canada where they were used by the French as slaves. The constant threat of Native American attacks kept the New Hampshire settlers from **expanding** into new areas. Food **production** dropped. Nearly every white family in New Hampshire suffered a loss.

## NEW HAMPSHIRE FIGHTS BACK

England could not afford to send the large numbers of soldiers required to fight the French and their Native American allies. As a result, New Hampshire and the other colonies had to provide their own soldiers to fight for the land. Several forts were built in New Hampshire to provide protection for the colony.

New Hampshire's settlers murdered thousands of Native Americans and burned their villages and crops. Even Native Americans who weren't involved in the fighting lost their lives and homes. A reward was offered for the **scalps** of Native American men, women, and children.

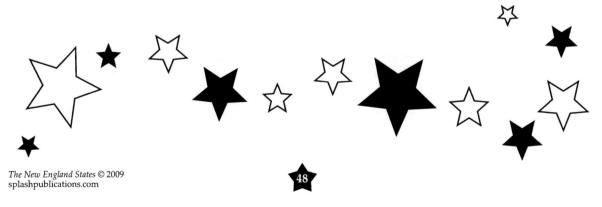

## HANNAH DUSTIN

Hannah Dustin lived with her husband and eight children in the New Hampshire town of Haverhill. In the spring of 1697, Native Americans raided Haverhill. They killed about 30 people and took several prisoners.

Hannah, her newborn baby, and the baby's nurse were taken as prisoners during the raid. Shortly after leaving Haverhill, the Native Americans murdered Hannah's baby.

The Native Americans and their captives traveled more than 100 miles through New Hampshire. They planned to take their prisoners to Canada and sell them as slaves to the French. The group stopped to rest along the Merrimack River.

Hannah and two other captives grabbed the hatchets of the sleeping Native Americans. They killed and scalped ten of the Native Americans. Hannah and the other surviving prisoners took a canoe and paddled down the Merrimack River to safety.

HANNAH DUSTIN

## FRANCE SURRENDERS

The French and Indian War was the final battle of a long conflict between France and the English colonists. In 1760, the French and their Native American allies finally surrendered. France signed a treaty and gave up all of its land east of the Mississippi River. In New Hampshire, the end of the war meant that the Native Americans were no longer a threat. Most of the surviving Native Americans moved out of New Hampshire. The area was opened to white settlement and the population of New Hampshire grew.

## GREAT BRITAIN'S UNFAIR TAXES

The English colonists faced a new enemy after the French and Indian War. Great Britain taxed the colonists to pay for an army and navy to protect the new land won during the war. Colonists were forced to pay taxes on imported items like sugar, tea, glass, paint, and paper. The colonists especially hated the Stamp Act. The Stamp Act required the colonists to buy stamps and stick them on legal documents and newspapers.

The colonists complained about "taxation without representation." Each colony had been careful to set up laws that allowed freedom of religion and self-government. They felt it was unfair for Parliament (PAR•luh•ment), 3,000 miles away in Great Britain, to tax them without their permission. The colonists believed that only the people they elected had the power to tax them. They argued that they did not elect any of the representatives in Parliament.

# THE REVOLUTIONARY WAR

The colonists accused Great Britain of trying to take away their freedom and liberty. The colonists made it clear that they were willing to fight for their independence.

In 1775, the first shots of the Revolutionary War were fired. Although no battles were fought on New Hampshire's soil, the people of New Hampshire played an important role in the struggle for independence.

Before the Revolutionary War started, New Hampshire began to form groups of minutemen. The minutemen were trained to fight a battle on a moment's notice.

New Hampshire's minutemen proved they were ready as they fought in the battles of Lexington and Concord in Massachusetts.

Many men from New Hampshire volunteered to fight in the Continental Army. Portsmouth was an important port from which about 100 **privateers** attacked British ships.

MINUTEMAN

# THE SECOND CONTINENTAL CONGRESS

After a year of fighting, delegates of the Second Continental Congress met in Philadelphia. The delegates decided that the colonies should declare their independence from Great Britain. In June 1776, the Second Continental Congress set up a committee of five men to write a statement of independence.

The committee members were John Adams, Thomas Jefferson, Benjamin Franklin, Roger Sherman, and Robert Livingston. Thomas Jefferson was chosen to write the document. Two weeks later, Jefferson finished the statement of independence.

# THE DECLARATION OF INDEPENDENCE

On July 2, 1776, the Second Continental Congress met to debate Jefferson's document. In his statement, Jefferson accused King George III of taking away the rights of the American colonists. Jefferson also attacked slavery and the slave trade. The representatives from the Southern states owned slaves. They refused to approve the document unless the part about slavery was taken out. After many hours of arguing, it was agreed that slavery would not be mentioned in the declaration.

Long before the Declaration of Independence was adopted and signed, New Hampshire had already taken its own steps toward independence. In January 1776, New Hampshire became the first of the 13 original colonies to form its own government.

In July 1776, the 13 original colonies adopted the Declaration of Independence. Together they formed the United States of America. The Revolutionary War was far from over.

In 1781, Great Britain surrendered the war to the Americans. Fighting continued in some areas for two more years. In 1783, British troops finally left the United States. A peace treaty was signed between the United States and Great Britain a few months later. Five years later, on June 21, 1788, New Hampshire became the ninth state to join the Union.

**THOMAS JEFFERSON**

# NEW HAMPSHIRE'S ECONOMY

**B**y the beginning of the 1800s, New Hampshire had **recovered** from the Revolutionary War. The state's economy was **prospering**. Farming, **commerce**, fishing, and lumbering were the main industries. Also important were manufacturing and the production of cotton goods, shoes, and wood products.

During the 1800s, more states joined the Union. In the 1820s, slavery became an angry issue between Northern states like New Hampshire, and the Southern states. The Northern states wanted to abolish slavery and make it **illegal** to own slaves. Although some Northerners owned slaves, the Northern states did not depend on slaves like the Southern states did. The economy in the North was based on manufacturing, not on farming. The Southern states, on the other hand, needed slaves. Their economy was based on tobacco and cotton farming. They used thousands of slaves to work on their huge plantations.

# THE CIVIL WAR

In 1861, the Civil War broke out. The United States was separated over the issue of slavery. Eleven Southern states seceded from the Union and formed their own nation, the Confederate States of America. The **Confederacy** elected its own president and made slavery legal. The Northern states were angry that the Southern states had split from the Union. For four long years, the Confederacy and the Union battled against one another. In 1865, the war ended and slavery was abolished. It took another five years before the United States became one nation again.

#  NEW HAMPSHIRE

**Directions:** Read each question.
Darken the circle for the correct answer.

**Directions:** Darken the circle for the word or words that give the meaning of the underlined word.

1  **After reading about New Hampshire's points of interest, you learn that –**

A  there aren't any high mountains in New Hampshire

B  New Hampshire borders the Pacific Ocean

C  more than half of New Hampshire is covered with trees

D  it never snows in New Hampshire

2  **In the third paragraph about John Smith, the word <u>expedition</u> means –**

F  Native American language

G  accident

H  a quick way of doing something

J  a journey for the purpose of exploring

3  **According to the information about Sir Edmund Andros, you get the idea that he was –**

A  well liked by the colonists

B  feared by the colonists

C  hated by the colonists

D  not a real person

4  **During King William's War, what kept the colonists from settling in other areas of New Hampshire?**

F  They liked where they lived.

G  They were too poor to move.

H  They feared Native American attacks.

J  Great Britain did not permit them to settle in other areas of New Hampshire.

5  **During the summer, the Pennacook traveled to the <u>seacoast</u> for fishing and gathering shellfish. <u>Seacoast</u> means –**

A  the shore of the sea

B  the bottom of the sea

C  a river

D  the top of the mountain

6  **Martin Pring explored the shoreline and a small area of New Hampshire's <u>interior</u>. <u>Interior</u> means –**

F  top

G  inside

H  big

J  outside

7  **The Northern states wanted to abolish slavery and make it <u>illegal</u>. <u>Illegal</u> means –**

A  secret

B  against the law

C  expensive

D  unable to find

8  **By the beginning of the 1800s, New Hampshire's economy was <u>prospering</u>. <u>Prospering</u> means –**

F  failing

G  protecting from danger

H  having success

J  arguing

**READING**

**Answers**

1  Ⓐ Ⓑ Ⓒ Ⓓ     5  Ⓐ Ⓑ Ⓒ Ⓓ
2  Ⓕ Ⓖ Ⓗ Ⓙ     6  Ⓕ Ⓖ Ⓗ Ⓙ
3  Ⓐ Ⓑ Ⓒ Ⓓ     7  Ⓐ Ⓑ Ⓒ Ⓓ
4  Ⓕ Ⓖ Ⓗ Ⓙ     8  Ⓕ Ⓖ Ⓗ Ⓙ

**Directions:** Here is a concept web to help you write a report about New Hampshire's famous people. Study the concept web and use it to answer questions 1-4.

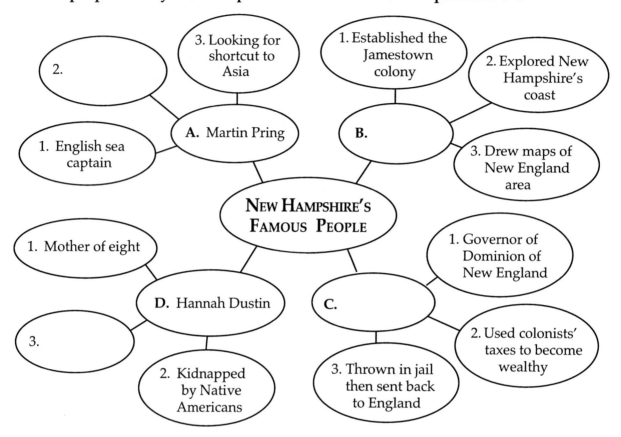

1   **Which of these belongs in number 2 around circle A?**

   **A** New Hampshire's first European visitor

   **B** First president of the United States

   **C** King of England

   **D** Spanish explorer

2   **Which of these belongs in circle B?**

   **F** Thomas Jefferson

   **G** King James II

   **H** Abraham Lincoln

   **J** John Smith

3   **Which of these belongs in circle C?**

   **A** John Adams

   **B** Benjamin Franklin

   **C** Sir Edmund Andros

   **D** Samuel de Champlain

4   **Which of these belongs in number 3 around circle D?**

   **F** Fought in the Revolutionary War

   **G** Killed and scalped ten Native Americans before escaping

   **H** George Washington's wife

   **J** Made the first American flag

LANGUAGE

**Answers**

1 Ⓐ Ⓑ Ⓒ Ⓓ     3 Ⓐ Ⓑ Ⓒ Ⓓ

2 Ⓕ Ⓖ Ⓗ Ⓙ     4 Ⓕ Ⓖ Ⓗ Ⓙ

Name _____

You just finished answering questions about a Concept Web of New Hampshire's famous people. In this activity, you will create your own Concept Web about New Hampshire. In a Concept Web, the topic is in the middle and information about the topic forms a "web." Use what you have read about New Hampshire to fill in the circles with the information requested.

**NEW HAMPSHIRE'S POINTS OF INTEREST**

**IMPORTANT DATES IN NEW HAMPSHIRE'S HISTORY**

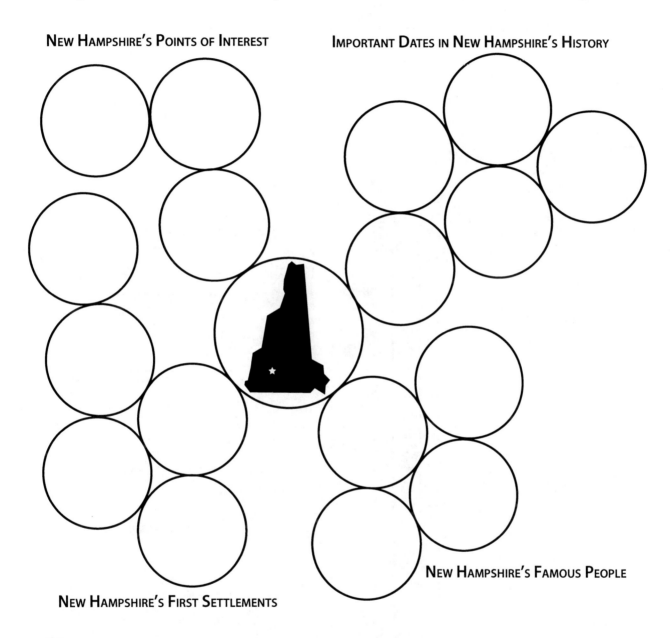

**NEW HAMPSHIRE'S FAMOUS PEOPLE**

**NEW HAMPSHIRE'S FIRST SETTLEMENTS**

Use the information from your Concept Web to write a rough draft four sentence paragraph about New Hampshire on the back of this paper. Your paragraph should include information about New Hampshire's points of interest, first settlements, famous people, and important dates. Start your paragraph with a Topic Sentence and don't forget to end it with a good Closing Sentence. Have your paragraph edited before neatly writing your final draft on separate paper.

# ☆ ★ ☆ ★★☆ Vocabulary Quiz ☆ ★ ☆ ★★☆
## New England States
### Part IV

**Directions:**  Match the vocabulary word on the left with its definition on the right.  Put the letter for the definition on the blank next to the vocabulary word it matches.  Use each word and definition only once.

1. _____ boundaries

2. _____ scalps

3. _____ captive

4. _____ recovered

5. _____ commerce

6. _____ province

7. _____ Confederacy

8. _____ prospering

9. _____ production

10. _____ council

11. _____ privateers

12. _____ destructive

13. _____ livestock

14. _____ interior

15. _____ illegal

A.  buying and selling a large amount of goods between different places.

B.  the act of making something.

C.  against the law.

D.  the tops of human heads that are usually covered with hair.

E.  causing harm.

F.  a hard rock containing crystals that was formed over millions of years.

G.  a part of a country having a government of its own.

H.  extremely cold area that looks like ice.

I.  the 11 states that separated from the United States in 1860 and 1861.

J.  a journey for the purpose of exploring.

16. _____ granite

17. _____ glacial

18. _____ formations

19. _____ expedition

20. _____ founded

21. _____ expanding

K. growing larger.

L. started or established.

M. a prisoner who has been taken by force without permission.

N. a group of people chosen to make laws or give advice.

O. animals that are raised on a farm to eat or sell for profit.

P. dividing lines.

Q. private ships with weapons that are licensed to attack enemy ships.

R. arrangements of something.

S. inside; away from a border or shore.

T. gotten back or regained.

U. having success or wealth.

# RHODE ISLAND

**R**hode Island, known as Little Rhody or the Ocean State, is the smallest of six New England states located in the Northeast region of the United States. In fact, with a land area of only 1,212 square miles, Rhode Island is the smallest state in the Union. Rhode Island was one of the 13 original colonies in America. It was also the last of the original 13 colonies to **ratify** the United States Constitution. This makes Rhode Island the 13th state.

The nickname Little Rhody was chosen because of its small size. However, the Ocean State is Rhode Island's **official** nickname. Rhode Island's location on the Atlantic Ocean makes it easy to understand the reason for this nickname.

The capital of Rhode Island is Providence. Providence is the third largest city in all of New England. Providence is a manufacturing city that produces silver, jewelry, and electronic equipment. It calls itself the Costume Jewelry Capital of the Nation.

The state bird of Rhode Island is the Rhode Island Red. The state flower is the Violet, and the state tree is the Red Maple. Rhode Island's motto is "Hope."

## RHODE ISLAND'S POINTS OF INTEREST

Rhode Island's cool summers have attracted visitors to its seashores for many years. With more than 400 miles of coastline, it is easy to understand why water sports are so popular in this small state. Rhode Island has been the favorite vacation spot for wealthy families since the end of the Civil War. These yearly travelers built mansions on the ocean that have since been turned into museums. The museums are open for public tours.

Newport, one of Rhode Island's most famous resort areas, features **annual yacht** races and one of the world's most famous jazz festivals. The Tennis Hall of Fame and Tennis Museum are also located in Newport. Rhode Island's visitors also enjoy many state parks, national monuments, and historic sites.

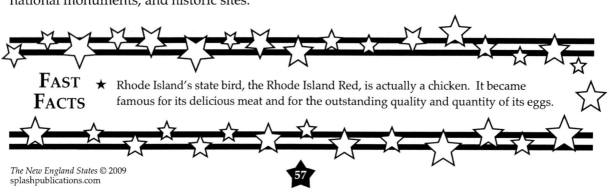

**FAST FACTS** ★ Rhode Island's state bird, the Rhode Island Red, is actually a chicken. It became famous for its delicious meat and for the outstanding quality and quantity of its eggs.

# RHODE ISLAND'S FIRST PEOPLE

Five Native American tribes that spoke the Algonquian (al•GONG•kee•in) language inhabited Rhode Island before Europeans visited the area. The largest and most powerful group was the Narragansett (nar•ra•GAN•set) tribe. About 5,000 members of this tribe lived in eight different villages throughout Rhode Island.

Other Native Americans in Rhode Island included the Niantic (nye•AN•tick), Wampanoag (wam•puh•NO•ag), Pequot (PEE•kwat), and the Nipmuc (NIP•muck). These Native Americans farmed, hunted deer, fished, and gathered shellfish from the Atlantic Ocean.

# ROGER WILLIAMS

Roger Williams was an important part of Rhode Island's history. He was not the first European to visit Rhode Island, but he did establish the first permanent settlement in the area.

**ROGER WILLIAMS**

Roger Williams was a Puritan preacher who lived in the Massachusetts Bay Colony. Like others, he traveled to America in search of religious freedom. He did not agree with the leadership of the Massachusetts Bay Colony and he refused to be quiet about it. Williams did not think the government should tell people how to practice their religion. He firmly believed that Puritans should not be able to start a colony in North America until they purchased the land from the Native Americans.

In 1635, Roger Williams was ordered to leave Massachusetts. At first he refused, but he found out that a group of men were coming to send his family and him back to England. He left his wife and two daughters in Massachusetts and went to Rhode Island.

Roger Williams was welcomed by the leader of the Wampanoag tribe. The Native Americans gave him food and shelter. After learning their ways and their language, he bought land from them.

In 1636, Williams and a few followers began building a town on the land purchased from the Wampanoag tribe. He quickly learned that the land was already claimed by the Plymouth Colony in Massachusetts. He did not want to cause trouble between the Plymouth Colony and the Massachusetts Bay Colony. Instead, he purchased nearby land from the Narragansett tribe. It was here that he started Rhode Island's first permanent settlement.

Roger Williams named the settlement Providence. Providence means God's guidance. He chose this name because he felt God had provided a place for him and others to worship freely. Providence was the first colony to welcome people of all religions and **nationalities**. As a result, Rhode Island was the site of the first Jewish **synagogue** (SIN•uh•gog), the first Baptist church, and one of the first **Quaker** meeting houses.

# ANNE HUTCHINSON

Roger Williams was not the only colonist who had difficulties in Massachusetts. While Williams was busy building his colony in Rhode Island, Anne Hutchinson was being arrested for speaking out in Massachusetts.

Anne Hutchinson was born in England. She arrived in Boston, Massachusetts at the age of 43. Like Roger Williams, Anne Hutchinson and her family traveled to America in search of religious freedom. She quickly found that the church run by the Massachusetts Bay Colony offered less religious freedom than the churches in England.

In Massachusetts, Anne quickly became a town leader. She nursed the sick and helped deliver babies. Hutchinson had 15 children of her own. Anne Hutchinson also led church meetings in her home. It was during these meetings that she caused the most trouble for the Puritan church.

It was believed that leading church meetings was a man's job. Women were supposed to keep quiet during church services and look after their children. She taught other women that they could pray to God without the help of a preacher. This went completely against the laws of the Puritan church.

In 1638, Anne Hutchinson was forced to leave the Massachusetts Bay Colony. With her family and a small group of followers, she traveled to Rhode Island. Roger Williams helped the group purchase land from the Native Americans in Rhode Island's present-day city of Portsmouth.

Anne continued her message in Portsmouth. She held church meetings in her home and taught colonists that God's love was for everyone. After her husband died, Anne moved to New York. In 1643, she was murdered by Native Americans.

**ANNE HUTCHINSON**

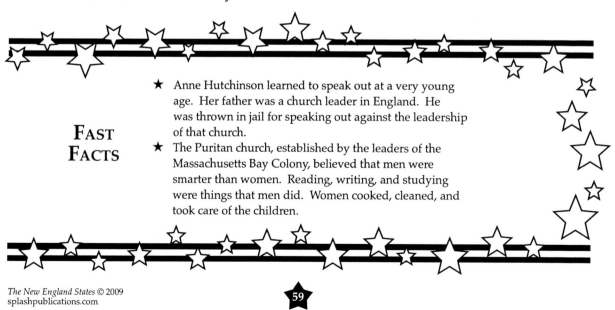

**FAST FACTS**

★ Anne Hutchinson learned to speak out at a very young age. Her father was a church leader in England. He was thrown in jail for speaking out against the leadership of that church.

★ The Puritan church, established by the leaders of the Massachusetts Bay Colony, believed that men were smarter than women. Reading, writing, and studying were things that men did. Women cooked, cleaned, and took care of the children.

# KING PHILIP'S WAR

Until 1675, Rhode Island's settlers had a peaceful relationship with the Native Americans. This was the year of King Philip's War. King Philip's War was the most destructive war in the history of the New England colonists. It was also disastrous for the Native Americans who participated in the war.

King Philip's War actually started after members of the Wampanoag tribe killed some cattle owned by the English colonists. The colonists allowed their cattle to roam freely and they trampled the corn crops of the Native Americans. The owner of the cattle responded by killing one of the Native Americans.

King Philip, a powerful Wampanoag chief, led his people in a **revolt** against the colonists. The Native Americans burned many New England towns and captured colonists.

The English colonists from Connecticut and Massachusetts were stronger than King Philip and his troops. They captured King Philip's wife and son and sold them into slavery. In the end, the colonists marched into Rhode Island and burned a Narragansett village.

More than 600 Narragansett men, women, and children were killed during the raid. The colonists from Rhode Island did not help the colonists from Massachusetts and Connecticut, but they didn't stop them either.

**KING PHILIP**

The Native Americans were angry with the Rhode Island colonists for allowing this to happen. King Philip joined forces with the Narragansett. Before the Native Americans could be defeated, 12 of Rhode Island's towns were completely destroyed and more than 1,000 colonists were killed.

In 1676, King Philip was hunted down and killed. Many of the surviving Native Americans were sold into slavery. Their land in Rhode Island was taken over by the colonists. This allowed more settlers to move into Rhode Island.

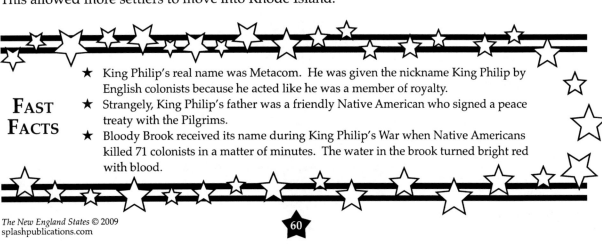

**FAST FACTS**

★ King Philip's real name was Metacom. He was given the nickname King Philip by English colonists because he acted like he was a member of royalty.
★ Strangely, King Philip's father was a friendly Native American who signed a peace treaty with the Pilgrims.
★ Bloody Brook received its name during King Philip's War when Native Americans killed 71 colonists in a matter of minutes. The water in the brook turned bright red with blood.

## INDEPENDENCE AND RHODE ISLAND'S STATEHOOD

On May 4, 1776, one month before the Declaration of Independence was adopted, Rhode Island boldly declared itself independent of Great Britain. It was among the first to declare its independence, but the last of the 13 original colonies to ratify the **federal** Constitution and join the United States.

Many farmers in Rhode Island were afraid to become part of the United States. They feared that they would lose the independence they had fought for during the Revolutionary War. Also, Rhode Island was against slavery. The Constitution of the United States allowed some states to own slaves. After much debate, and a vote of 34 to 32, Rhode Island finally agreed to join the Union. On May 29, 1790, Rhode Island became the 13th state.

## RHODE ISLAND'S ECONOMY

After statehood, Rhode Island's population more than doubled to 175,000. This growth came about because of the industries that developed in Rhode Island. In 1790, Samuel Slater produced a machine for spinning cotton. Settlers soon came from other states to own and work in Rhode Island's textile mills. During the 1800s, jewelry and silverware manufacturing were also important to Rhode Island's economy.

## THE CIVIL WAR

During the Civil War, more than 20,000 men from Rhode Island fought to abolish slavery in the South. This may seem odd, because Rhode Island needed to buy cotton from the plantation owners in the South. Slaves were used on the plantations to grow the cotton. The cotton was used to make products in Rhode Island's textile mills. If slavery was abolished, the Southern cotton farmers would not be able to produce cotton for Rhode Island's textile mills. Fighting to end slavery might hurt Rhode Island's economy.

After the Civil War ended, the slaves were set free. Many of the Southern plantation owners found it difficult to run their huge farms without the help of slaves. As a result, less cotton was available for Rhode Island's textile mills. Rhode Island solved its problem by using wool in its textile mills instead of cotton. Wool came from sheep and slave labor was not needed for this.

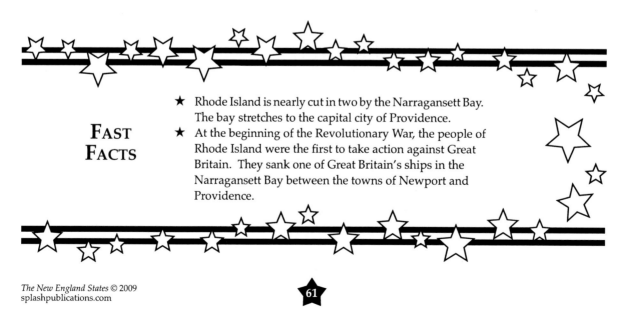

**FAST FACTS**

★ Rhode Island is nearly cut in two by the Narragansett Bay. The bay stretches to the capital city of Providence.
★ At the beginning of the Revolutionary War, the people of Rhode Island were the first to take action against Great Britain. They sank one of Great Britain's ships in the Narragansett Bay between the towns of Newport and Providence.

# RHODE ISLAND

**Directions:** Read each question.
Darken the circle for the correct answer.

**Directions:** Darken the circle for the word that has the same or almost the same meaning as the underlined word.

1  **According to the first paragraph, why is the number 13 important to Rhode Island?**

   A  There are 13 stripes and 13 stars on Rhode Island's state flag.

   B  Rhode Island became a state on the 13th day of the month.

   C  Rhode Island was one of the 13 original colonies and the 13th state to ratify the Constitution.

   D  There are 13 states smaller than Rhode Island.

2  **Which words about Roger Williams show that he felt strongly about his beliefs?**

   F  ...refused to be quiet about it...

   G  ...purchased the land...

   H  ...established the first permanent settlement...

   J  ...bought land from them...

3  **According to the information about Anne Hutchinson, what got her in the most trouble?**

   A  She nursed the sick.

   B  She helped deliver babies.

   C  She had 15 children of her own.

   D  She led church meetings.

4  **Which statement about King Philip's War is true?**

   F  The war started because the Native Americans were angry with King Philip.

   G  Rhode Island's colonists helped the Native Americans win the war.

   H  King Philip's wife and son were captured during the war.

   J  After the war, King Philip moved to Connecticut.

5  **Annual** means –

   A  weekly

   B  monthly

   C  yearly

   D  daily

6  A **yacht** is a –

   F  large house

   G  laugh

   H  sailboat used for racing

   J  plant that grows in warm regions

7  A **synagogue** is a –

   A  dangerous disease

   B  place of worship

   C  woven or knit cloth

   D  story passed down from the past

8  **official** means –

   F  wrong

   G  correct

   H  quick

   J  tired

9  **mansions** are –

   A  small rocks

   B  people

   C  stacks of books

   D  huge homes

**READING**

**Answers**

1  Ⓐ Ⓑ Ⓒ Ⓓ          6  Ⓕ Ⓖ Ⓗ Ⓙ
2  Ⓕ Ⓖ Ⓗ Ⓙ          7  Ⓐ Ⓑ Ⓒ Ⓓ
3  Ⓐ Ⓑ Ⓒ Ⓓ          8  Ⓕ Ⓖ Ⓗ Ⓙ
4  Ⓕ Ⓖ Ⓗ Ⓙ          9  Ⓐ Ⓑ Ⓒ Ⓓ
5  Ⓐ Ⓑ Ⓒ Ⓓ

**Directions: Read each sentence carefully. Then darken the circle for the correct answer to each question.**

Here is a rough draft letter written by King Philip to his Wampanoag tribe. Read the rough draft carefully. Then answer questions 1-4.

---

April 12, 1675

My Dear People,

(1) I am writing to you because I need your help. (2) The white strangers are taking the land that belongs to our friends. (3) The Narragansett. (4) My wife and son have been kidnapped. (5) I'm not sure where the white strangers have taken them. (6) I must find them and bring them home after I find them. (7) I hope we can depend upon our white friends from the nearby towns to help us. (8) Please join with me in battle against our enemies.

Your beloved chief,
Philip

---

**1** Which sentence best combines sentences 2 and 3 without changing their meaning?

  **A** Our friends, the Narragansett, are taking over the land that belongs to the white strangers.

  **B** Taking over the land that belongs to our friends, the white strangers are.

  **C** The white strangers are taking over the land that belongs to our friends, the Narragansett.

  **D** Strangers are the whites and friends are the Narragansett.

**2** Which sentence needlessly repeats a word or group of words?

  **F** 1
  **G** 4
  **H** 6
  **J** 8

**3** Which group of words is <u>not</u> a complete sentence?

  **A** 2
  **B** 3
  **C** 7
  **D** 8

**4** What is the best way to write sentence 8?

  **F** Please join with me battling against our enemies.

  **G** Our enemies need to be battled against, please join me.

  **H** Join me, battle against our enemies, they need it.

  **J** As it is written.

---

**LANGUAGE**

**Answers**

1 Ⓐ Ⓑ Ⓒ Ⓓ    3 Ⓐ Ⓑ Ⓒ Ⓓ
2 Ⓕ Ⓖ Ⓗ Ⓙ    4 Ⓕ Ⓖ Ⓗ Ⓙ

**G**eography is the study of the Earth. It includes the Earth's land, water, weather, animal life, and plant life. **Geographers** are people who study geography. You can think of yourself as a geographer because you will be learning about places on the Earth.

**Location** is important to the study of geography. It is almost impossible to figure out your location or find your way around if you do not know the four main, or **cardinal directions.** North, south, east, and west are the **cardinal directions**. On a map these directions are labeled N, S, E, and W.

**COMPASS ROSE**

Between the four main directions are the **intermediate directions.** Northeast, or NE, is the direction between north and east. Southeast, or SE, is the direction between south and east. Southwest, or SW, is the direction between south and west. Northwest, or NW, is the direction between north and west.

A **reference point** is also important for finding your location. A **reference point** is simply a starting point. It's difficult, for example, to travel north if you don't have a starting point.

**Example:**  Sugarloaf is a ski resort in the winter and a golfer's paradise in the summer. From the first winter snowfall until early May, visitors enjoy skiing and snowboarding down the second highest mountain in the state. During the summer months, the snow melts and Sugarloaf turns into one of this state's most popular golf courses. Sugarloaf is <u>north</u> of <u>Augusta</u>.

This example gives you some very important information. It tells you that your **reference point,** or starting point, will be the city of Augusta. Locate Augusta on your New England States map. Put your finger on Augusta and slide it <u>north</u>. You should see a picture of Sugarloaf already placed there for you.

Sometimes directions contain more than one **reference point**. Look at the example below:

**Example:** Wright Museum preserves the history of World War II, a six year period from 1939 to 1945, when our country was at war with Germany, Italy, Japan, and their allies. Wright Museum features World War II tanks, jeeps, fighter planes, and many **artifacts** important to the war. Wright Museum is <u>northeast</u> of <u>Concord</u> and <u>southwest</u> of Augusta.

This example contains two **reference points** and two sets of directions. They have been underlined for you. Look at your New England States map. Put your finger on the city of Concord and slide it <u>northeast</u>. Since there are many points of interest located northeast, a second **reference point** has been added to help you find your location.

The second **reference point** is Augusta. Place your finger on Augusta and slide it <u>southwest</u>. By using both of these **reference points**, you should be able to easily locate Wright Museum.

**Directions:** In this activity you will use reference points, cardinal directions, and intermediate directions to plot important points of interest on a New England States map. Many of these points of interest preserve history. This helps historians learn more about the people who lived before us.

1. Use your scissors to carefully cut out the symbols on the bottom of the last page.

2. Label the cardinal and intermediate directions on the compass rose drawn for you on the New England States map.

3. Use the written directions and your compass rose to correctly locate these points of interest on your New England States map.

4. To get you started, the reference points and directions have been underlined for you in the first five descriptions. You may want to underline the reference points and directions in the rest of the activity.

5. Glue the symbols in their proper places on your map. (Glue the symbols right over the dots.)

6. When you have finished, neatly label each New England state with its correct name. Use your coloring pencils to add color to your New England States map.

1. Fairbanks Museum and **Planetarium** was opened in 1891. It was one of the first teaching museums in America. The museum is home to this state's only public planetarium and weather gallery. Fairbanks Museum and Planetarium is <u>northwest</u> of <u>Wright Museum</u>.

2. Whaleback Light is a lighthouse that was built in 1872. It is made of unpainted granite blocks topped with a light that flashes every 10 seconds to safely guide sailors into the harbor. A fog signal blasts from Whaleback Light every 30 seconds. The lighthouse keeper lives inside the 50 foot tower. Whaleback Light is <u>south</u> of <u>Augusta</u>.

3. Cape Cod National Seashore features historic buildings, lighthouses, and a beach that stretches for 40 miles. Cape Cod National Seashore is <u>southeast</u> of <u>Whaleback Light</u>.

4. The New England Aquarium is home to more than 70 **exhibits** of animals from around the world. The four-story, 200,000 gallon Giant Ocean Tank, features a coral reef with sharks, turtles, and thousands of smaller fish. Other exhibits feature penguins, lobsters, and a live whale birth. The New England Aquarium is <u>southeast</u> of <u>Concord</u> and <u>northwest</u> of <u>Cape Cod National Seashore</u>.

5. Quechee **Gorge** is this state's "Little Grand Canyon." Though it is only 165 feet deep, the Quechee Gorge offers visitors one of the best canyons in New England. Hikers who want to view the waterfall at the bottom of the canyon can complete the 1.6 mile trip into and out of the gorge in about one hour. Quechee Gorge is <u>southwest</u> of <u>Fairbanks Museum and Planetarium</u> and <u>northwest</u> of <u>Concord</u>.

6. Acadia National Park was the first national park built east of the Mississippi River. The park is home to many different types plants and animals. Peregrine falcons can be seen soaring high above Cadillac Mountain, the highest point on the Atlantic Coast. Acadia National Park is southeast of Sugarloaf.

7. The Harriet Beecher Stowe Center preserves the life and work of famous **abolitionist** and author, Harriet Beecher Stowe. It was Stowe's book, *Uncle Tom's Cabin,* that made people want to help slaves escape to freedom. During her lifetime, Harriet Beecher Stowe raised seven children and published 30 books. The Harriet Beecher Stowe Center is west of Providence.

8. Moosehorn National Wildlife **Refuge** was established in 1937, as a safe place for birds and other wildlife. In recent years, three pairs of bald eagles have nested at Moosehorn. Black ducks, wood ducks, ring-necked ducks, Canadian geese, and loons can also be seen on the refuge's 50 lakes. Moosehorn National Wildlife Refuge is northeast of Acadia National Park.

9. Pillsbury State Park is a heavily wooded area with more than 50 miles of hiking and mountain biking trails. Visitors to this quiet park enjoy canoeing, fishing, hiking, and exploring the history of an early farm settlement that was located here during the late 1700s. Pillsbury State Park is northeast of Quechee Gorge and west of Wright Museum.

10. Beartown State Forest is two different places in the summer and winter. During the warm summer months, swimmers, boaters, and hikers enjoy the park. They wait quietly to view deer, bears, bobcats, and other wild animals in their natural **habitats**. During the winter months, Beartown State Forest becomes a winter wonderland where skiers and snowmobile riders can explore the snow covered **wilderness**. Beartown State Forest is northwest of the Harriet Beecher Stowe Center.

11. Milan State Park is known for fishing, canoeing, **kayaking,** and wildlife viewing. From this hilltop campground, visitors get a complete view of the mountain ranges in New Hampshire, Maine, Vermont, and Canada. Milan State Park is west of Sugarloaf.

12. Shelburne Falls Bridge of Flowers is the only flower-covered bridge in the world. It features over 500 **varieties** of flowers, vines, and shrubs that bloom from April to October. The flowers are grown and maintained through **donations** and the hard work of volunteers. Shelburne Falls Bridge of Flowers is northeast of Beartown State Forest.

**13.** Martha's Vineyard was established in 1642. Its location on the Atlantic Ocean makes it a favorite spot for boating, swimming, biking, and catching a delicious lobster for dinner. Martha's Vineyard is southeast of Providence.

**14.** Baxter State Park is a wilderness area of 202,064 acres. The land was given to this state by one of its governors, Percival P. Baxter. The park offers more than 175 miles of trails for summer hikers. During the winter, the trails are covered with a blanket of snow and hiking boots are traded for cross country skis. Baxter State Park is located north of Acadia National Park.

**15.** Rosie O'Grady's Balloon of Peace Monument marks the starting point for the world's first **solo** balloon flight across the Atlantic Ocean. In 1984, Joe Kittinger flew 3,535 miles from this spot to Italy in his hot air balloon named *Rosie O' Grady's Balloon of Peace*. Rosie O'Grady's Balloon of Peace Monument is located northeast of Baxter State Park.

**16.** Beardsley Zoological Gardens is this state's only zoo. Visitors stroll through 52 acres set aside for wild animals from North and South America. Beardsley Zoological Gardens is located southwest of the Harriet Beecher Stowe Center.

Quechee Gorge

Acadia National Park

Harriet Beecher Stowe Center

Moosehorn National Wildlife Refuge

Pillsbury State Park

Beartown State Forest

Milan State Park

Shelburne Falls Bridge of Flowers

Martha's Vineyard

Baxter State Park

Rosie O'Grady's Balloon of Peace Monument

Beardsley Zoological Gardens

Name _____

# NEW ENGLAND STATES

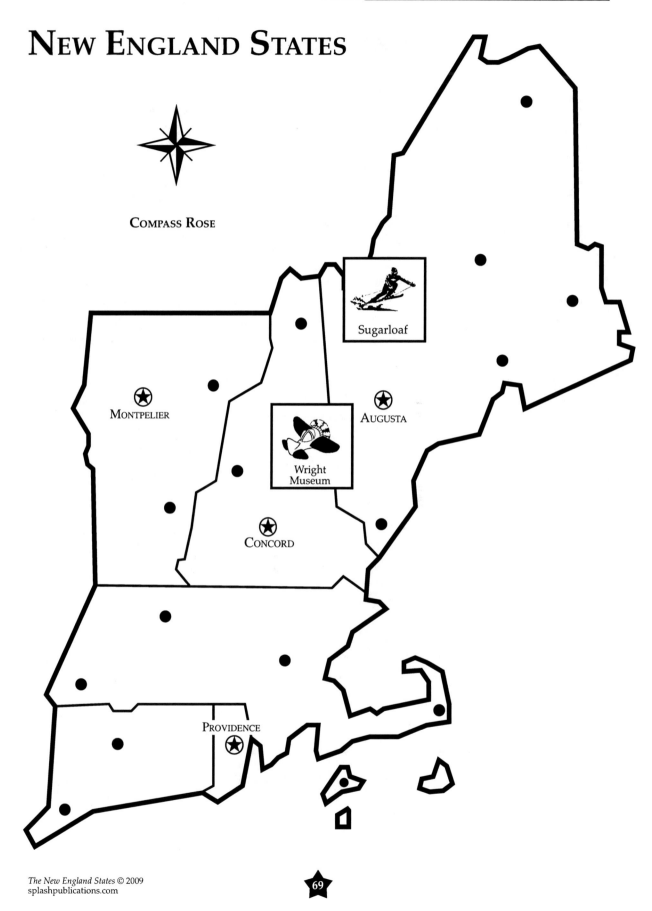

COMPASS ROSE

Sugarloaf

MONTPELIER

AUGUSTA

Wright
Museum

CONCORD

PROVIDENCE

# VERMONT

Vermont, the Green Mountain State, is a New England state located in the Northeast region of the United States. The name Vermont comes from two French words that mean "green" and "mountain." The Green Mountains are a thick forest of pine, spruce, beech, birch, and sugar maple trees covering most of the state.

Montpelier (mont•PEEL•yer) is the capital of Vermont. This city is located in the Green Mountains. Montpelier is named after the French city of Montpellier (mont•pee•YEAH). The economy of Montpelier centers around insurance companies, manufacturing, and **tourism** from nearby ski resorts.

The state bird of Vermont is the Hermit Thrush. The state flower is the Red Clover, and the state tree is the Sugar Maple. Vermont's motto is "Freedom and Unity."

## VERMONT'S POINTS OF INTEREST

Vermont is a beautiful state with a rich history. The highways in Vermont are dotted with more than 1,200 historic site markers. The Shelburne Museum contains one of the largest collections of American History in the country. Old Constitution House in the city of Windsor was the site of the signing of Vermont's first state constitution.

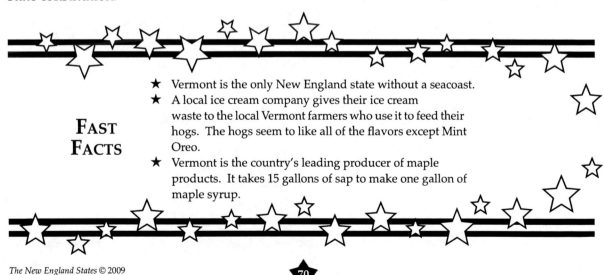

**FAST FACTS**

★ Vermont is the only New England state without a seacoast.
★ A local ice cream company gives their ice cream waste to the local Vermont farmers who use it to feed their hogs. The hogs seem to like all of the flavors except Mint Oreo.
★ Vermont is the country's leading producer of maple products. It takes 15 gallons of sap to make one gallon of maple syrup.

## RECREATION IN VERMONT

Vermont's cool **climate** and mountain lakes also attract visitors in both winter and summer. With over 15 major downhill ski resorts, snow skiing is a popular sport in Vermont. The Craftsbury Nordic Center is a world class ski area that is also used as a training facility for the United States Olympic cross-country skiing team.

More than half of Vermont is covered by forestland. As a result, Vermont has many state forests and state parks. The Green Mountain National Forest offers visitors thousands of acres of hiking trails.

Maple syrup lovers enjoy the fact that one of Vermont's most valuable products is the thick brown syrup that comes from the sugar maple trees growing throughout the state.

## CONTROL OF VERMONT

In 1609, French explorer Samuel de Champlain (sham•PLANE) arrived in Vermont. He traveled by way of the lake that he named after himself, Lake Champlain. Champlain found Native Americans of Algonquian (al•GONG•kee•in) and Iroquois (EAR•uh•kwoy) tribes living in and using Vermont for hunting and fishing. Champlain claimed Vermont for France. For the next 150 years, the French, the English, and the Native Americans battled for control of Vermont.

In 1666, the French built Fort St. Anne. The French tried to control the land along Lake Champlain, but the settlement failed. In 1724, the English colonists from the Massachusetts Bay Colony built Fort Dummer to protect their people in the Connecticut Valley. This was the first permanent settlement in Vermont. Fort Dummer gave the English colonists control over the region.

The English permanently controlled Vermont after the French and Indian War. Because France lost the war, it had to give all of its land east of the Mississippi River to Great Britain. This included the French-controlled territory in Vermont.

## VERMONT'S BOUNDARY DISPUTES

There were still many **disputes** over the boundaries of Vermont. The Massachusetts Bay Colony, and the governors of New Hampshire and New York all claimed to own parts of Vermont. Between 1749 and 1764, Governor Wentworth of New Hampshire sold land in southwestern Vermont to his citizens. Then, in 1764, Governor Clinton of New York sold the exact same land to his people. New Hampshire's settlers were very angry that people from New York were taking over the land in Vermont that they had settled. They were willing to fight for control of the land.

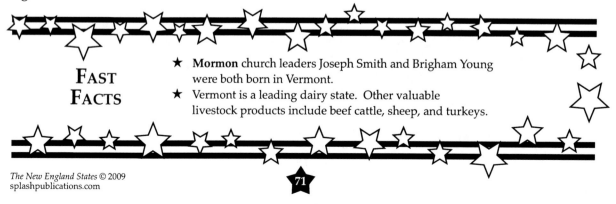

**FAST FACTS**

★ **Mormon** church leaders Joseph Smith and Brigham Young were both born in Vermont.
★ Vermont is a leading dairy state. Other valuable livestock products include beef cattle, sheep, and turkeys.

# THE GREEN MOUNTAIN BOYS

A group of 11 men organized themselves to protect Vermont's first settlers. Ethan Allen was chosen to be their leader. Allen first tried to settle the land disputes peacefully in court. When this didn't work, Ethan Allen gathered more than 200 men at a **tavern** in the town of Bennington. They named themselves the Green Mountain Boys and prepared for battle.

For the next two years, Ethan Allen and the Green Mountain Boys fought New Yorkers who tried to settle in Vermont. New Yorkers considered Ethan Allen and his men **outlaws**. They called them the Bennington Mob.

# THE REVOLUTIONARY WAR

In April 1775, the first shots of the Revolutionary War were fired. The Green Mountain Boys left Vermont and helped the minutemen during the battles of Lexington and Concord. After the battles of Lexington and Concord, the British Army remained in Boston. George Washington, the commander of the Continental Army, planned to drive the British troops out of Boston. To do this, the Continental Army needed **artillery**.

The British Army had hidden cannons in the colony of New York at Fort Ticonderoga (tie•con•duh•ROW•guh). On May 10, 1775, Colonel Benedict Arnold and his troops joined with Ethan Allen and the Green Mountain Boys to capture Fort Ticonderoga. Surprisingly, they took over the fort peacefully without firing a single shot.

A few days later, the Green Mountain Boys helped Benedict Arnold's troops successfully capture Crown Point, another British fort in New York. The

**ETHAN ALLEN**

cannons were heavy, and needed to be moved from New York to Boston. The Continental Army loaded the cannons onto sleds and pulled them across the snow-covered Berkshire Mountains.

It took three months to get the much needed artillery to Boston. After the Green Mountain Boys captured a British ship, the American colonists had complete control of the Champlain River Valley.

The Green Mountain Boys **convinced** the colonists to take them into the Continental Army. In 1775, during an attack on the city of Montreal (mon•tree•ALL) in Canada, Ethan Allen was captured by British troops. He spent more than two years in a British prison. Benedict Arnold was seriously wounded during the battle. The Americans failed to take over Canada.

## THE BATTLES OF SARATOGA

Seth Warner took command of the Green Mountain Boys. With the help of the Continental Army, Seth Warner led the Green Mountain Boys in several Revolutionary War victories. One of the biggest victories for the Green Mountain Boys and the Continental Army came during the Battles of Saratoga. During the summer of 1777, Great Britain planned to send troops from Canada to capture New York's Hudson River Valley. This would split the United States into two parts and make it weaker. New England would be cut off from the rest of the colonies. The colonists wouldn't be able to get men and supplies from New England. Great Britain hoped that this would defeat the American armies once and for all.

General John Burgoyne (bur•GOIN) was the commander of the British Army. He was not prepared for the Continental Army and the Green Mountain Boys. Burgoyne reached the town of Saratoga in New York. His army of 6,000 men was outnumbered by the American troops. After several **vicious** (VIH•shus) battles, Burgoyne was forced to surrender. The Americans took nearly 6,000 British prisoners and a large supply of weapons. The victories in the Battles of Saratoga convinced the French to enter the war on the side of the Americans.

## VERMONT BECOMES A STATE

In the middle of the Revolutionary War, a group of Vermont residents declared their independence from Great Britain. They met to set up a state that would be separate from New York. In July of 1777, the citizens of Vermont adopted a state constitution. This was the first American constitution to **forbid** slavery. It also gave all adult males, not just those who owned property, the right to vote.

Vermont asked the Continental Congress to accept its constitution and recognize it as a state. The Congress refused because of the boundary disputes with New York.

Vermont tried very hard to become independent from New York. Vermont made its own money and established its own government. Vermont even made plans to include some of the border towns in New Hampshire and New York as part of its state. Finally, in 1790, New York agreed to give up its control of Vermont. Vermont paid New York $30,000 for this land. Congress was satisfied. On March 4, 1791, Vermont became the 14th state to join the Union.

## VERMONT'S ECONOMY

The population of Vermont expanded greatly after it became a state. By 1810, there were more than 215,000 people living in Vermont. Most of the new settlers came from other New England towns to farm wheat. Others arrived in Vermont to work in industries that produced textiles, iron, lumber, and **potash**.

In 1825, the Erie Canal opened. Many people left Vermont and moved to Ohio where they found better farmland. Ohio was located on the Erie Canal. Farmers could make more money selling their products by shipping them down the canal.

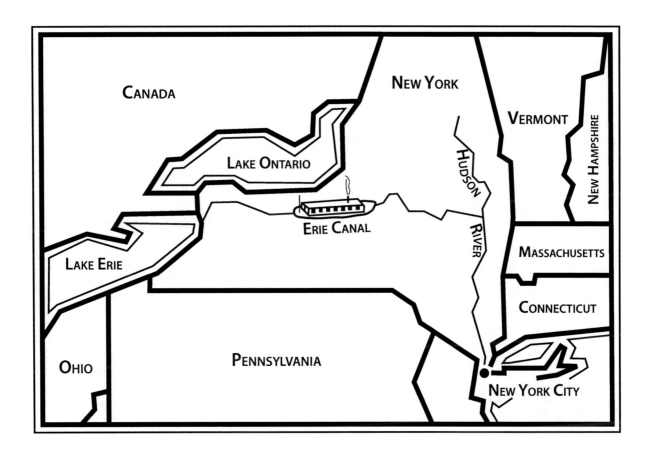

## THE CIVIL WAR

During the Civil War, about 35,000 men from Vermont fought against the South in an effort to end slavery and bring the United States back together. No major battles were fought in Vermont, but the state did have a bit of excitement.

In October 1864, a group of Confederate soldiers from Canada entered the northern part of Vermont. They stole $200,000 from the town's banks. Soldiers chased and caught the bank robbers as they entered Canada. Less than half of the money was ever found.

Name _____

**Directions:** Read each question. Darken the circle for the correct answer.

**Directions:** Darken the circle for the sentence that uses the underlined word in the same way as the sentence in the box.

---

**1**    Vermont is known as the –

   **A**   Ocean State

   **B**   Green Mountain State

   **C**   Red Clover State

   **D**   Bay State

**2**    According to the Fast Facts at the bottom of the first page, Vermont is the only state without a –

   **F**   nickname

   **G**   river

   **H**   seacoast

   **J**   museum

**3**    After reading about Vermont's boundary disputes, you learn that –

   **A**   nobody wanted to claim Vermont

   **B**   Vermont was sold to different groups of people at the same time

   **C**   there were no boundary disputes in Vermont

   **D**   settlers from New York were welcomed into Vermont

**4**    What can you learn by studying the map of the Erie Canal?

   **F**   The Erie Canal is south of Pennsylvania.

   **G**   The Erie Canal is north of Lake Ontario.

   **H**   The Erie Canal is southwest of Vermont.

   **J**   The Erie Canal runs through the center of Massachusetts.

---

**5** | The economy of Montpelier <u>centers</u> around insurance companies, manufacturing, and tourism. |

In which sentence does <u>centers</u> have the same meaning as the sentence above?

   **A**   I only like the <u>centers</u> of the cookies.

   **B**   We have Reading <u>centers</u> at school.

   **C**   Please cut out the <u>centers</u> of the circles.

   **D**   His day <u>centers</u> around work and school.

**6** | More than half of Vermont is <u>covered</u> by forestland. |

In which sentence does <u>covered</u> have the same meaning as the sentence above?

   **F**   My brother was <u>covered</u> in mud.

   **G**   I <u>covered</u> the cake to keep it fresh.

   **H**   The <u>covered</u> wagons traveled West.

   **J**   We <u>covered</u> that in class yesterday.

**7** | During the 1700s, many people claimed to own <u>part</u> of Vermont. |

In which sentence does <u>part</u> have the same meaning as the sentence above?

   **A**   My hair has a <u>part</u> down the middle.

   **B**   We were missing <u>part</u> of the game.

   **C**   I have to <u>part</u> with my favorite toys.

   **D**   The car won't run without a new <u>part</u>.

---

**READING**

**Answers**

1  Ⓐ Ⓑ Ⓒ Ⓓ    5  Ⓐ Ⓑ Ⓒ Ⓓ

2  Ⓕ Ⓖ Ⓗ Ⓙ    6  Ⓕ Ⓖ Ⓗ Ⓙ

3  Ⓐ Ⓑ Ⓒ Ⓓ    7  Ⓐ Ⓑ Ⓒ Ⓓ

4  Ⓕ Ⓖ Ⓗ Ⓙ

# VERMONT

**Directions: Read each sentence carefully. Then darken the circle for the correct answer to each question.**

Here is a rough draft paragraph about Ethan Allen. There are certain words and phrases underlined. Read the rough draft carefully. Then answer questions 1-5.

---

### ETHAN ALLEN

(1) Ethan Allen was born on <u>January 10 1738</u>. (2) He was <u>the older child</u> in a family with seven children. (3) In 1755, while Ethan was planning to go to college, his father died. (4) Ethan was left to care for <u>the familys farm</u>. (5) Ethan went on to marry Mary Brownson. (6) The couple had five children before Mary died of tuberculosis. (7) Before becoming the leader of the famous Green Mountain Boys, Ethan Allen served in the <u>French and Indian War</u>. (8) His protection of Vermont's early settlers earned him a place in <u>the states history</u>.

---

**1** In sentence 1, <u>January 10 1738</u> is best written –

   A   January, 10 1738
   B   january 10, 1738
   C   January 10, 1738
   D   As it is written.

**2** In sentence 2, <u>the older child</u> is best written –

   F   the most old child
   G   the oldest child
   H   the older children
   J   As it is written.

**3** In sentence 4, <u>the familys farm</u> is best written –

   A   the families farm
   B   the family's farm
   C   the familys' farm
   D   As it is written.

**4** In sentence 7, <u>French and Indian War</u> is best written –

   F   French and indian War
   G   french and Indian War
   H   French and Indian war
   J   As it is written.

**5** In sentence 8, <u>the states history</u> is best written –

   A   the state's history
   B   the States history
   C   the states' history
   D   As it is written.

---

**LANGUAGE**

**Answers**

1  Ⓐ Ⓑ Ⓒ Ⓓ    4  Ⓕ Ⓖ Ⓗ Ⓙ
2  Ⓕ Ⓖ Ⓗ Ⓙ    5  Ⓐ Ⓑ Ⓒ Ⓓ
3  Ⓐ Ⓑ Ⓒ Ⓓ

# ☆☆☆☆ THE AMERICAN REVOLUTION ☆☆☆☆

**T**he American Revolution was a period of great change in our nation's history. You may think that the Revolutionary War started because the English colonists simply wanted to be free of Great Britain's control. Actually, the fighting started long before the first shots were fired.

Imagine for a moment that you were an English colonist living during the 1700s. You were trying to be successful in the New World, but you were constantly battling against the French and their Native American allies for control of land and beaver hunting territories. The leaders in Great Britain demanded that you and other colonists stand up and fight. That's exactly what you did.

## THE FRENCH AND INDIAN WAR

**F**or most of the 1700s, you and other colonists like you fought against the French and their Native American allies. Great Britain even helped by sending soldiers and supplies so you could win the battle. Finally, in 1763, the French and Indian War ended. France and their Native American allies were defeated. Great Britain took control of all French land east of the Mississippi River. You and other English colonists throughout the 13 original colonies celebrated. You returned to farming, hunting, fishing, and taking care of your family.

## GREAT BRITAIN'S TAXES

**U**nfortunately, that wasn't the end of it. The French and Indian War created more problems. It was expensive for Great Britain to send all of those soldiers and supplies to help you and the other colonists win the war. Somebody had to pay for this debt. Great Britain decided that colonists like yourself should be responsible. After all, you were living in America. Great Britain's citizens couldn't be expected to pay the debt for protecting your land.

The leaders in Great Britain decided to raise the money it was owed through taxes. Everyday items like stamps, sugar, paper, paint, and tea suddenly became more expensive to buy. Not only did you have to pay the regular price of these items, now you had to pay a few cents extra. All of the "extra" money was sent back to Great Britain to pay off your debt.

# GREAT BRITAIN GOES TOO FAR

You and your friends didn't like the idea of being taxed by Great Britain. Since arriving in America, you colonists had been free to choose your own leaders, make your own laws, and decide when and how things should be taxed. Who did the leaders in Great Britain think they were?

To make things worse, those British soldiers who helped fight the French and Indian War were sticking around. Once again, Great Britain's leaders decided that you colonists should provide the soldiers with food and shelter.

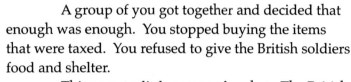

A group of you got together and decided that enough was enough. You stopped buying the items that were taxed. You refused to give the British soldiers food and shelter.

Things got a little messy after that. The British soldiers went a little crazy and killed five **innocent** colonists in the town of Boston. Great Britain backed off a little after this. The British soldiers were removed from Boston until things cooled down. Most of the taxes were removed too. Except, of course, the tax on tea. You colonists loved your tea. You were so mad about the tea tax that you dumped an entire shipload of British tea into the Boston Harbor. Oops!

# THE DECISION THAT CHANGED HISTORY

The leaders in Great Britain weren't going to let you colonists get away with this. They demanded that you pay for the tea. The Boston Harbor was locked until the bill for the tea was paid. In addition, King George III took away your freedom to make laws and choose your own leaders.

That was the last straw. A group of you got together again and decided that the colonists had no choice but to fight. You had risked everything to come to America where you could live freely. Now you faced the possibility of being under the control of Great Britain's leaders, 3,000 miles away. The time had come to fight for complete independence from Great Britain.

Name _____

# ⭐ CAUSE AND EFFECT ⭐

In history, the _effect_ from one event often _causes_ another event. For example, you could say that the disagreements over slavery and the separation of the South from the Union _caused_ the Civil War. One _effect_ of the Civil War was that slavery was abolished.

---

Directions: Use the selection about the American Revolution to answer these _cause_ and _effect_ questions. Circle the answers to questions 1 and 2. Write your answers on the lines provided for questions 3-6.

---

1   According to the selection, what _caused_ the French and Indian War?

    A  Disagreements over slavery.

    B  Control of land and hunting territories.

    C  Failure of the colonists to pay taxes to Spain.

    D  The desire for complete independence from Great Britain.

2   According to the selection, what was one _effect_ of the French and Indian War?

    A  The British soldiers returned to Great Britain.

    B  Great Britain's leaders gave the colonists large sums of money for winning the war.

    C  Great Britain took control of all French land east of the Mississippi River.

    D  Slavery was abolished and the United States became whole again.

3   What _caused_ Great Britain to tax the colonists for everyday items like stamps, sugar, paper, paint, and tea?

_____

_____

4   What was one _effect_ of these taxes?

_____

_____

5   What _caused_ the colonists to dump a shipload of British tea into the Boston Harbor?

_____

_____

6   What was the _effect_ of dumping the tea into the Boston Harbor?

_____

_____

# NEW ENGLAND RIDDLER

**L**earning about different places is important to the study of geography. Describing a place can help you learn how places are similar and different from one another. In this activity, you will solve riddles based on the place descriptions of the six New England states in the Northeast region. Remember, these states include Connecticut, Maine, Massachusetts, New Hampshire, Rhode Island, and Vermont.

**Directions:** Use your written information about each of the six New England states to solve the 10 riddles. Every state will be used at least once. Some of the states will be used more than once. Be careful to read the entire clue before deciding which state <u>best</u> answers the question, "Who Am I?" Write your answers on the lines provided.

**1.** My state capital is also my second largest city and an important manufacturing area. My visitors enjoy more than 100 state parks. Hikers challenge themselves on the Appalachian Trail, which crosses through my western side. My first English settlers came from a colony in Massachusetts and built the Three River Towns.

### Who Am I ? _____

**2.** Most of my land is covered with woods where deer, black bears, moose, and bobcats live. I only take up 10,000 square miles of space, making me one of the smallest states in the Union. My nickname comes from the fact that there are so many granite formations and deposits located within me. One of my most famous sites is the "Old Man of the Mountain," a rock formation that looks like a human face.

### Who Am I ? _____

**3.** I have a land area of 1,212 square miles. I am bordered on the south by the Atlantic Ocean, and as a result I have more than 400 miles of coastline. This probably explains why they call me the Ocean State. My state capital is a manufacturing city and the third largest city in all of New England.

### Who Am I ? _____

**4.** A river runs through my middle and divides me in half. The river is enjoyed by visitors who like fishing, boating, and swimming. Public beaches on Long Island Sound border me on the south and separate me from the state of New York. One of my points of interest is home to mammals and exotic birds.

## Who Am I ? _____

**5.** I am the least populated state east of the Mississippi River. My southeastern coast is formed by the Atlantic Ocean. Most of my 33,215 square miles are covered with thick forests. My forests are home to many types of animals and more than 300 species of birds.

## Who Am I ? _____

**6.** My first English settlers came from Massachusetts to build a colony along the Kennebec River in my present-day city of Augusta. This area was full of thick forests, and the settlers made money by cutting down my trees and selling lumber. I am proud of the fact that I have at least 5,000 rivers and streams and more than 2,500 lakes and ponds.

## Who Am I ? _____

**7.** My state capital is the largest city in all of New England and the region's most important seaport. I am covered by more than three million acres of forestland. The Blue Hills is a popular recreation area in my state. Before the beginning of the Revolutionary War, my harbor was full of British tea.

## Who Am I ? _____

**8.** I love the color purple. My state bird is the Purple Finch and my state flower is the Purple Lilac. My visitors enjoy camping, hiking, and skiing in my White Mountains. My southeastern corner dips into the Atlantic Ocean, so visitors to my coastline enjoy sandy beaches. My capital city manufactures electronic equipment and leather.

## Who Am I ? _____

**9.** I am a beautiful state with a rich history. My name comes from two French words that mean "green" and "mountain." I am the only New England state without a seacoast. My state tree is the sugar maple, and I am popular for producing maple syrup.

## Who Am I? _____

**10.** My visitors enjoy both land and water. Summer visitors travel to my elbow-shaped peninsula where they stay at my famous resorts on Cape Cod. Winter visitors enjoy skiing down my slopes in the Berkshire Hills. I also have over 150 national historic sites.

## Who Am I? _____

List two ways that the New England states are similar to one another.

**1.** _____

_____

**2.** _____

_____

List two ways that the New England states are different from one another.

**1.** _____

_____

**2.** _____

_____

Name _____

**Directions:**     Match the vocabulary word on the left with its definition on the right.  Put the letter for the definition on the blank next to the vocabulary word it matches.  Use each word and definition only once.

1. _____ artillery

2. _____ yacht

3. _____ climate

4. _____ synagogue

5. _____ convinced

6. _____ revolt

7. _____ disputes

8. _____ ratify

9. _____ Quaker

10. _____ exhibits

11. _____ official

12. _____ nationalities

13. _____ forbid

14. _____ Mormon

15. _____ outlaws

A.   a sailboat used for racing.

B.   a small canyon with a stream running through it.

C.   groups of people from different countries.

D.   a fight against authority.

E.   building where images of stars and planets are projected onto a dome-shaped ceiling.

F.   people who break the law.

G.   displays.

H.   large weapons like cannons or rockets.

I.   traveling through water in a boat that looks like a canoe.

J.   a chemical made from wood ashes and used as vitamins in soil.

K.   proper or correct.

L.   alone.

M.   talked into.

N.   not guilty.

O.   someone who belonged to a religious group that believed all men were created equal.  They refused to serve in the army or navy and would not pay taxes used to support war.

16. _____ potash

17. _____ federal

18. _____ annual

19. _____ tavern

20. _____ tourism

21. _____ vicious

22. _____ abolitionist

23. _____ donations

24. _____ gorge

25. _____ habitats

26. _____ innocent

27. _____ kayaking

28. _____ planetarium

29. _____ refuge

30. _____ solo

31. _____ varieties

32. _____ wilderness

33. _____ artifacts

P.  a bar or restaurant where alcoholic beverages are served.

Q.  a place of worship for people of the Jewish religion.

R.  a person who belongs to a religious group that was founded in 1830, and traces its beginnings to Joseph Smith.

S.  an unsettled area where wild animals live.

T.  arguments or disagreements.

U.  objects and tools used by early humans for eating, cooking, and hunting.

V.  places where plants and animals grow or live in nature.

W.  the business of providing services for people who are on vacation.

X.  a person who wanted to end slavery.

Y.  evil and violent behavior.

Z.  an event that takes place once each year.

AA.  to give legal approval by voting.

BB.  free gifts given to someone in need.

CC.  a system of government (like the United States) in which the power is shared between the national and state governments.

DD.  shelter or protection from danger.

EE.  many different kinds.

FF.  the average weather conditions of a place over a period of years.

GG.  to order not to do something.

# NEW ENGLAND
## STATES AND CAPITALS QUIZ

You have completed your study of the New England states. You are now ready to take a quiz on the New England states and their capitals.

**Directions:** Label each of the six New England states on the map below. Use the lines provided to fill in each state's capital city. Spelling Counts!

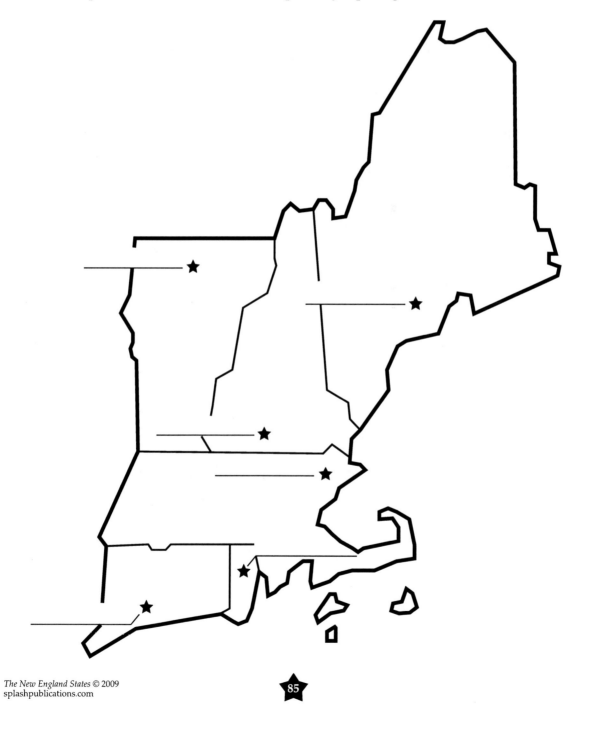

# GLOSSARY

**a•bol•ished** stopped or put an end to.

**a•bo•li•tion•ist** a person who wanted to end slavery.

**ac•cused** blamed or charged with a crime.

**a•dop•ted** accepted and put into action.

**ag•ri•cul•ture** planting crops and raising farm animals.

**al•lies** groups of people who come together to help one another in times of trouble.

**A•mer•i•can Rev•o•lu•tion** conflict between 13 English colonies in North America and their mother country, Great Britain. Also known as the Revolutionary War.

**am•mu•ni•tion** bullets and explosive items used in war.

**an•nu•al** an event that takes place once each year.

**an•ti•slav•er•y** against slavery.

**ap•point•ed** chosen or selected.

**ar•ti•facts** objects and tools used by early humans for eating, cooking, and hunting.

**ar•til•ler•y** large weapons like cannons or rockets.

**au•to•bi•og•ra•phy** the story of your life written by you.

**Ber•mu•da** a British colony located in the Atlantic Ocean.

**bi•og•ra•phies** stories of a person's life written by someone else.

**bor•ders** lies right next to something.

**bound•a•ries** dividing lines.

**boy•cot•ting** refusing to buy.

**brand•ed** burned a mark into the skin of a person or animal. During the early days of history, this was used for criminals to easily identify them as law breakers.

**ca•nal** a man-made waterway for boats or for watering crops.

**cap•i•tal** the city that serves as the center of government for the state.

**cap•tive** a prisoner who has been taken by force without permission.

**char•ter** a contract which gives one group power over another.

**cit•i•zens** people living in a city, town, state, or country who enjoy the freedom to vote and participate in government decisions.

**cli•mate** the average weather conditions of a place over a period of years.

**coast** an area of land that borders water.

**col•o•nies** groups of people who are ruled by another country.

**col•o•nists** people who live in a colony.

**com•merce** buying and selling a large amount of goods between different places.

**com•pro•mise** an agreement reached when each side changes or gives up some of its demands.

**con•fed•er•a•cy** a group of people with common goals.

**Con•fed•er•a•cy** the 11 states that separated from the United States in 1860 and 1861.

**Con•fed•er•ate States of A•mer•i•ca** the nation formed by the Southern states during the Civil War.

**con•flict** a struggle or disagreement.

**con•quered** defeated by force.

**con•sti•tu•tion** a plan which outlines the duties of the government and guarantees the rights of the people.

**Con•ti•nen•tal Ar•my** American troops that fought against Great Britain during the Revolutionary War.

**Con•ti•nen•tal Con•gress** the group of leaders from the 13 original colonies who had the power to make laws and decisions for the newly formed United States.

**con•trast** to show the differences.

**con•vinced** talked into.

**coun•cil** a group of people chosen to make laws or give advice.

**de•bate** a discussion that gives arguments for and against a subject.

**debt** money that is owed to someone else.

**de•feat•ed** won victory over.

**del•e•gates** people sent with power to represent others.

**de•struc•tive** causing harm.

**de•vot•ed** promised to be loyal to something.

**dis•guised** changed appearance to keep from being recognized.

**dis•putes** arguments or disagreements.

**do•min•ion** large territory with one ruler.

**do•na•tions** free gifts given to someone in need.

**e•con•o•my** the way a city, state, or country makes money.

**e•lec•tions** selections of leaders by voting for them.

**En•gland** a region located on the southern part of the island of Great Britain.

**Eu•ro•pe•ans** people who come from the continent of Europe.

**e•vac•u•at•ed** removed people from a place of danger.

**ex•hib•its** displays.

**ex•ot•ic** strange, unusual, rare.

**ex•pand•ing** growing larger.

**ex•pe•di•tion** a journey for the purpose of exploring.

**ex•plo•ra•tions** trips taken for the purpose of discovering something.

**fed•er•al** a system of government (like the United States) in which the power is shared between the national and state governments.

**fer•til•ized** added a material to the soil to make crops grow better.

**flee** to run away from danger.

**for•bid** to order not to do something.

**for•ma•tions** arrangements of something.

**found•ed** started or established.

**ge•og•ra•phy** the study of the Earth.

**gla•cial** extremely cold area that looks like ice.

**gorge** a small canyon with a stream running through it.

**gov•er•nor** a person who is in charge of an area or group.

**gran•ite** a hard rock containing crystals that was formed over millions of years.

**Great Bri•tain** the largest island in Europe. It includes England, Scotland, and Wales.

**Great Lakes** five large lakes located in North America at the border between Canada and the United States. The names of the lakes are Superior, Michigan, Huron, Erie, and Ontario.

**hab•i•tats** places where plants and animals grow or live in nature.

**har•bor** a sheltered area of water deep enough to provide ships a place to anchor.

**harsh** very uncomfortable conditions.

**his•to•ri•ans** people who study history.

**hos•til•i•ty** anger.

**il•le•gal** against the law.

**im•port•ed** brought items into a country for the purpose of selling them.

**in•de•pen•dent** not under the control or rule of another.

**in•dus•tries** businesses that provide a certain product or service.

**in•hab•it•ed** lived or settled in a place.

**in•no•cent** not guilty.

**in•te•ri•or** inside; away from a border or shore.

**in•tol•er•a•ble** unbearable.

**is•land** land surrounded on all sides by water.

**kay•ak•ing** traveling through water in a boat that looks like a canoe.

**li•ber•ty** freedom to do as one pleases.

**live•stock** animals that are raised on a farm to eat or sell for profit.

**loy•al** faithful.

**maize** Native American corn.

**mam•mals** warm-blooded animals who feed their young with milk, have backbones, and are covered with hair.

**man•sion** huge home.

**man•u•fac•tur•ing** making something from raw materials by hand or machinery.

**mas•sa•cre** the violent and cruel killing of a large number of people.

**mer•chants** buyers and sellers who do so for profit.

**mi•li•tia** a group of men having some military training who are called upon only in emergencies.

**min•ute•men** groups of armed men who were prepared to fight on a minute's notice during the Revolutionary War.

**mon•u•ments** buildings, stones, or statues created to remember a person or event.

**Mor•mon** a person who belongs to a religious group that was founded in 1830, and traces its beginnings to Joseph Smith.

**moth•er coun•try** original homeland of the English colonists.

**mot•to** a short phrase describing conduct or principles.

**mus•kets** guns that are loaded through the muzzle.

**na•tion•al•i•ties** groups of people from different countries.

**Ne•ther•lands** an independent European country bordered by the North Sea, Belgium, and Germany.

**New En•gland** an area in the northeast United States that includes the states of Connecticut, Maine, Massachusetts, New Hampshire, Rhode Island, and Vermont.

**New France** the part of North America claimed by France from the early 1600s until 1763.

**New World** a term once used to describe the continents of North and South America.

**North A•mer•i•ca** one of seven continents in the world. Bounded by Alaska in the northwest, Greenland in the northeast, Florida in the southeast, and Mexico in the southwest.

**of•fi•cial** proper or correct.

**out•laws** people who break the law.

**o•ver•thrown** removed from power.

**Par•lia•ment** the group of people in Great Britain that makes the laws.

**pen•in•su•la** a piece of land extending into a body of water.

**Pil•grims** the English colonists who founded the first permanent settlement in New England at Plymouth in 1620.

**plan•e•tar•i•um** building where images of stars and planets are projected onto a dome-shaped ceiling.

**plan•ta•tions** very large farms in the South where crops of cotton and tobacco were grown and slave labor was generally used.

**pop•u•lat•ed** the number of people living in a place.

**po•tash** a chemical made from wood ashes and used as vitamins in soil.

**pre•served** protected from injury or ruin so more can be learned.

**pri•va•teers** private ships with weapons that are licensed to attack enemy ships.

**pro•duc•tion** the act of making something.

**prof•it•a•ble** a business that makes money.

**pros•per•ing** having success or wealth.

**pro•test** to argue against something believed to be unfair.

**prov•ince** a part of a country having a government of its own.

**Pu•ri•tan** a person from England who traveled to America in the 1600s and 1700s in search of religious freedom.

**Qua•ker** someone who belonged to a religious group that believed all men were created equal. They refused to serve in the army or navy and would not pay taxes used to support war.

**raid•ed** attacked suddenly.

**rat•i•fy** to give legal approval by voting.

**re•cov•ered** gotten back or regained.

**re•en•act•ment** to act or perform again.

**ref•uge** shelter or protection from danger.

**re•pealed** done away with; removed.

**rep•re•sen•ta•tives** people chosen to speak or act for an entire group.

**re•sort** a place where people go for a vacation.

**re•volt** a fight against authority.

**scalps** the tops of human heads that are usually covered with hair.

**sea•port** a port, harbor, or town within reach of seagoing ships.

**se•ced•ed** withdrew from the United States and formed a separate nation.

**so•lo** alone.

**spe•cies** groups of plants or animals that are alike in many ways.

**sur•ren•dered** gave up completely.

**sur•viv•al** continuing to live.

**sus•tains** keeps going without giving up.

**syn•a•gogue** a place of worship for people of the Jewish religion.

**ta•vern** a bar or restaurant where alcoholic beverages are served.

**ter•ri•to•ries** areas of land controlled by a person or group of people.

**tex•tile** a woven or knit cloth.

**tim•ber** wood used for building something.

**tour•ism** the business of providing services for people who are on vacation.

**trans•plant•ed** moved from one place and settled someplace else.

**trea•ty** a formal agreement.

**trol•ley** passenger vehicle that runs on railway tracks set in the street.

**Un•ion** coming together under one government, the way the United States did in 1776.

**u•nit•ed** came together and formed a single unit.

**va•ri•e•ties** many different kinds.

**ven•i•son** deer meat.

**vi•cious** evil and violent behavior.

**vic•to•ri•ous** having won a victory.

**vowed** promised.

**voy•ages** journeys that are usually made by water.

**wam•pum** beads made of shells that were once used for money or decoration by Native Americans.

**West In•dies** a chain of about 1,000 islands in the Caribbean Sea that stretches from the southern tip of Florida to the northeastern corner of South America.

**wil•der•ness** an unsettled area where wild animals live.

**yacht** a sailboat used for racing.

# ANSWERS

## ANSWERS TO COMPREHENSION QUESTIONS

### CONNECTICUT

READING
1. C
2. G
3. C
4. F
5. B
6. J
7. D
8. F

LANGUAGE
1. B
2. J
3. B
4. J
5. D
6. F

### MAINE

READING
1. D
2. F
3. B
4. G
5. A
6. F
7. D

LANGUAGE
1. B
2. G
3. C
4. G

### MASSACHUSETTS

READING
1. B
2. H
3. D
4. J
5. A
6. H
7. D

LANGUAGE
1. C
2. J
3. C
4. F
5. C

### NEW HAMPSHIRE

READING
1. C
2. J
3. C
4. H
5. A
6. G
7. B
8. H

LANGUAGE
1. A
2. J
3. C
4. G

### RHODE ISLAND

READING
1. C
2. F
3. D
4. H
5. C
6. H
7. B
8. G
9. D

LANGUAGE
1. C
2. H
3. B
4. J

### VERMONT

READING
1. B
2. H
3. B
4. H
5. D
6. F
7. B

LANGUAGE
1. B
2. G
3. B
4. J
5. A

### CAUSE AND EFFECT

1. B
2. C
3. Debt from the French and Indian War.
4. The taxes raised the price of items; Colonists refused to pay the taxes.
5. The tax on tea.
6. The Boston Harbor was locked and King George took away freedom of colonists to make their own laws.

# ANSWERS TO VOCABULARY QUIZZES

| PART I | PART II | PART III | PART IV | PART V |
|---|---|---|---|---|
| 1. H | 1. CC | 1. DD | 1. P | 1. H |
| 2. K | 2. Q | 2. K | 2. D | 2. A |
| 3. C | 3. D | 3. T | 3. M | 3. FF |
| 4. DD | 4. Z | 4. C | 4. T | 4. Q |
| 5. GG | 5. M | 5. X | 5. A | 5. M |
| 6. R | 6. G | 6. M | 6. G | 6. D |
| 7. JJ | 7. A | 7. P | 7. I | 7. T |
| 8. AA | 8. X | 8. E | 8. U | 8. AA |
| 9. W | 9. E | 9. II | 9. B | 9. O |
| 10. M | 10. HH | 10. I | 10. N | 10. G |
| 11. HH | 11. AA | 11. AA | 11. Q | 11. K |
| 12. N | 12. DD | 12. A | 12. E | 12. C |
| 13. D | 13. T | 13. FF | 13. O | 13. GG |
| 14. O | 14. II | 14. V | 14. S | 14. R |
| 15. S | 15. V | 15. B | 15. C | 15. F |
| 16. EE | 16. R | 16. HH | 16. E | 16. J |
| 17. T | 17. O | 17. R | 17. H | 17. CC |
| 18. BB | 18. I | 18. J | 18. R | 18. Z |
| 19. F | 19. EE | 19. JJ | 19. J | 19. P |
| 20. L | 20. N | 20. D | 20. L | 20. W |
| 21. Y | 21. B | 21. EE | 21. K | 21. Y |
| 22. FF | 22. W | 22. O | | 22. X |
| 23. CC | 23. K | 23. GG | | 23. BB |
| 24. KK | 24. GG | 24. F | | 24. B |
| 25. B | 25. L | 25. S | | 25. V |
| 26. J | 26. Y | 26. CC | | 26. N |
| 27. LL | 27. H | 27. H | | 27. I |
| 28. II | 28. S | 28. W | | 28. E |
| 29. X | 29. FF | 29. Z | | 29. DD |
| 30. I | 30. F | 30. L | | 30. L |
| 31. U | 31. U | 31. LL | | 31. EE |
| 32. P | 32. P | 32. U | | 32. S |
| 33. E | 33. BB | 33. Q | | 33. U |
| 34. A | 34. C | 34. BB | | |
| 35. Q | 35. JJ | 35. N | | |
| 36. V | 36. J | 36. KK | | |
| 37. Z | | 37. G | | |
| 38. G | | 38. Y | | |

# VENN DIAGRAM PARAGRAPH GRADING CHART

## PARAGRAPH CONTENT

| CRITERIA | POINTS POSSIBLE | POINTS EARNED |
|---|---|---|
| Topic Sentence | 15 | |
| Four Supporting Sentences with appropriate information from Graphic Organizer | 60 (15 points per sentence) | |
| Closing Sentence | 15 | |
| Neatness of Final Draft | 10 | |
| **TOTAL** | 100 | |

## PARAGRAPH MECHANICS

| CRITERIA | POINTS POSSIBLE | POINTS EARNED |
|---|---|---|
| Spelling | 20 | |
| Punctuation | 20 | |
| Grammar | 20 | |
| Capitalization | 20 | |
| Sentence Structure | 20 | |
| **TOTAL** | 100 | |

## ANSWERS TO CONSIDER THE SOURCE

1. P
2. P
3. S
4. P
5. S
6. P
7. S

# ANSWER TO MASSACHUSETTS GRID MATH

# ANSWERS TO NEW HAMPSHIRE CONCEPT WEB

### POINTS OF INTEREST
White Mountains
Old Man of the Mountain
Lost River
Mount Washington
Hampton Beach
Franklin Pierce Homestead
Daniel Webster Birthplace
Robert Frost Farm

### FIRST SETTLEMENTS
Dover
Exeter
Hampton
Portsmouth
Rye

### FAMOUS PEOPLE
Sir Edmund Andros
Samuel de Champlain
Hannah Dustin
Martin Pring
John Smith

### IMPORTANT DATES
1603-Martin Pring Visit
1605-Samuel de Champlain Visit
1614-John Smith Explorations
1623-First New Hampshire Settlements
1638-Portsmouth, Exeter, and Hampton Settlements
1680-Royal Colony
1686-Sir Edmund Andros's Arrival
1689-Andros Sent Back to England
1689-King William's War
1697-Hannah Dustin Kidnapped
1760-End of French and Indian War
1775-Revolutionary War Started
1776-Declaration of Independence
1781-Revolutionary War Ended
1788-New Hampshire Statehood
1861-Civil War Started
1865-Civil War Ended

## Paragraph Content

| CRITERIA | POINTS POSSIBLE | POINTS EARNED |
|---|---|---|
| Topic Sentence | 15 | |
| Four Supporting Sentences with appropriate information from Graphic Organizer | 60 (15 points per sentence) | |
| Closing Sentence | 15 | |
| Neatness of Final Draft | 10 | |
| **TOTAL** | **100** | |

## Paragraph Mechanics

| CRITERIA | POINTS POSSIBLE | POINTS EARNED |
|---|---|---|
| Spelling | 20 | |
| Punctuation | 20 | |
| Grammar | 20 | |
| Capitalization | 20 | |
| Sentence Structure | 20 | |
| **TOTAL** | **100** | |

## Answers to The New England States Riddler

1. Connecticut
2. New Hampshire
3. Rhode Island
4. Connecticut
5. Maine
6. Maine
7. Massachusetts
8. New Hampshire
9. Vermont
10. Massachusetts

Similarities: Forests, animals, Atlantic Ocean, beaches, mountains, hiking, camping, skiing.

Differences: Sizes, access to water, different rivers and mountain ranges, different points of interest.

# ANSWERS TO NEW ENGLAND STATES MAPPING

# ANSWERS TO NEW ENGLAND STATES & CAPITALS QUIZ

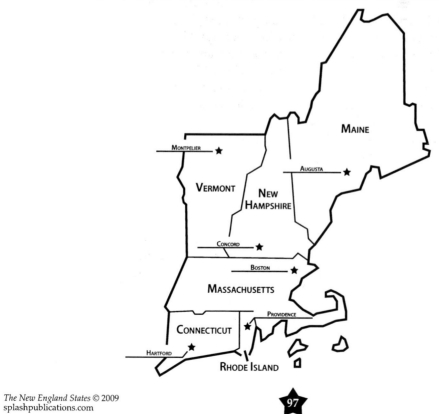

# BIBLIOGRAPHY

*American Heritage Dictionary of the English Language, Fourth Edition*, Houghton Mifflin, Massachusetts, 2000.

AmericanRevolution.com: 'The American Revolution' 2006 [Online]
Available <http://www.americanrevolution.com/> (December 17, 2008)

Bartleby: 'American Heritage Dictionary of the English Language: Fourth Edition' 2000 [Online]
Available <http://www.bartleby.com> (August 23, 2007)

Baranzini, Marlene and Bovert, Howard (1995), *US Kids History Book of the New American Nation*, Yolla Bolly Press, California

Carter, Alden R. (1988), *Birth of the Republic*, Frank Watts, New York

Davis, Kenneth (2001), *Don't Know Much about the 50 States!*, Harper Collins, USA

Fradin, Dennis (1990), *The Connecticut Colony*, Children's Press, Chicago

Fradin, Dennis (1987), *The Massachusetts Colony*, Regensteiner and Children's Press, Chicago

Fradin, Dennis (1988), *The New Hampshire Colony*, Children's Press, Chicago

Fradin, Dennis (1989), *The Rhode Island Colony*, Children's Press, Chicago

Fradin, Dennis (1995), *Rhode Island: From Sea to Shining Sea*, Children's Press, Chicago

Headley, Amy and Smith, Victoria. (2003), *Do American History!* Splash! Publications, Arizona

Holypark Media: 'Facts You May not Know about the Boston Tea Party' 2008 [Online]
Available <http://www.boston-tea-party.org/unknown-facts.html> (Februray 22, 2009)

Hooker, Richard: 'The Iroquois League' 1996 [Online]
Available <http://www.wsu.edu/~dee/CULAMRCA/IRLEAGUE.HTM> (January 2, 2009)

Houdman, M. and Matthews-Rose, R: 'The Mayflower Compact' 2008 [Online]
Available <http://www.allabouthistory.org/mayflower-compact.htm> (March 28, 2008)

Isaacs, Sally Senzell (1998), *America in the Time of Pocahontas*, Heinemann Library, Illinois

Internet School Library Media Center: 'Colonial America 1600-1775 K12 Resources' 2003 [Online]
Available <http://falcon.jmu.edu/~ramseyil/colonial.htm#A> (March 10, 2008)

Krull, Kathleen (1997), *Wish You Were Here: Emily's Guide to the 50 States*, Bantam Doubleday, New York

Landry, Peter: 'Samuel de Champlain' 1997 [Online] Available
<http://www.blupete.com/Hist/BiosNS/1600-00/Champlain.htm> (April 10, 2008)

Lexico Publishing Group: 'Dictionary.com' 2004 [Online]
Available <http:// dictionary.reference.com/> (September 1, 2008)

Lukes, Bonnie L. (1996), *The American Revolution*, Lucent Books, California

McNair, Sylvia (1999), *Connecticut: America the Beautiful*, Children's Press, New York

Museum of New France: 'The Explorers' 2000 [Online] Available
<http://www.civilization.ca/vmnf/explor/explor_e.html> (May 7, 2008)

New Hampshire Department of Resources and Economic Development: 'State Parks' 2008 [Online]
Available <http://www.visitnh.gov/why-new-hampshire/exploring-the-great-outdoors/state-parks.aspx> (June 2, 2008)

Nussbaum, Greg: 'Revolutionary War' 2005 [Online]
    Available <http://www.mrnussbaum.com/amflash.htm> (November 2, 2008)
Nussbaum, Greg: 'Samuel de Champlain' 2008 [Online] Available
    <http://www.mrnussbaum.com/champ2.htm> (February 3, 2009)
Parsons, Greg: 'New England Waterfalls: Queche Gorge, Vermont' 2002 [Online] Available
    <http://www.newenglandwaterfalls.com/waterfall.php?name=Quechee%20Gorge>
Shelburne Falls Area Business Association: 'Bridge of Flowers' 2008 [Online] Available
    <http://www.shelburnefalls.com/attractions/bridge.html> (June 30, 2008)
StateParks.com: 'Beartown State Forest' 2008 [Online] Available
    <http://www.stateparks.com/beartown.html> (January 20, 2009)
Steins, Richard (2000), *Exploration and Settlement*, Steck-Vaughn, Texas
Vermont Attractions Association: 'Visit Vermont's Best!' 2008 [Online] Available
    <http://www.vtattractions.org/index.php>
*Webster's Revised Unabridged Dictionary*, MICRA, New Jersey, 1998.
Woods, Mario (1997), *The World of Native Americans*, Peter Bedrick Books, New York
Worx Group, The: 'Harriet Beecher Stowe Center' 2005 [Online] Available
    <http://www.harrietbeecherstowecenter.org/index_home.shtml> (July 3, 2008)
Wright Museum: 'America at War, 1939-1945, the Home Front' 2003 [Online] Available
    <http://www.wrightmuseum.org/index.html> (June 1, 2008)